Boyology

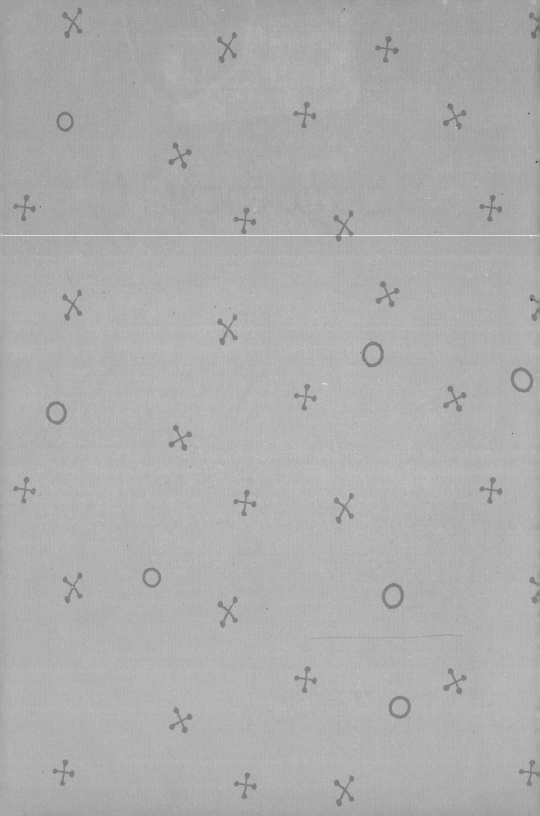

Boyology

a teen girl's crash course
in all things boy

By Sarah O'Leary Burningham
Illustrations by Keri Smith

chronicle books · san francisco

For Grant, the ultimate boyfriend —Sarah O'Leary Burningham

To protect teenagers who've shared their stories, some names have been changed.

Book design by Amelia May Anderson.
Typeset in Usherwood, Neutra, Slim Pickens, and Varsity Script.
The illustrations in this book were rendered digitally.
Manufactured in China.

Library of Congress Cataloging-in-Publication Data
Burningham, Sarah O'Leary.
Boyology : a teen girl's crash course in all things boy / by Sarah O'Leary Burningham ; illustrated by Keri Smith.
p. cm.
ISBN 978-0-8118-6436-7
1. Teenage boys—Psychology. 2. Teenage girls—Psychology.
3. Interpersonal relations in adolescence. I. Title.
HQ797.B77 2009
306.730835—dc22
2008005277

10 9 8 7 6 5 4 3 2 1

Chronicle Books LLC
680 Second Street, San Francisco, California 94107

www.chroniclekids.com

Contents

Welcome to the Wonderful World of Boys

Boys. Sometimes you think you've got them all figured out. Then they pull something like taking you paint-balling after prom, and you're back at square one. What gives?

The truth is, boys are as clueless as you are. They might act like they've got it together—at least they planned something for prom, right?—but just as you need a little help figuring them out, they could use a few clues in the girl department.

Remember *Romeo and Juliet*? No, seriously. Shakespeare may have died hundreds of years ago, but that guy understood relationships like no one else. Romeo sees Juliet at a party and thinks she's hot. He's too nervous to straight-up ask her out, so he sends one of his friends to find out about her. After he gets the dirt, he tracks her down, they start flirting, and it just gets hotter from there.

Note: If you missed the day your English class read *Romeo and Juliet*, check out the Claire Danes/Leonardo DiCaprio movie version. You'll get the idea—plus, they make a really cute couple, and the movie has a sweet retro soundtrack.

No wonder *Romeo and Juliet* has been popular for so long: Who *can't* relate to getting tripped up by romance? (At least until Juliet drinks the potion that makes her seem dead, and Romeo kills himself thinking he's lost her—that's a bit much.) If only Romeo and Juliet had communicated a little better, they might have lived happily ever after! Communication problems are nothing new. For centuries, men and women have found it challenging to relate to one another.

And it's easy to see why. You have countless questions about what he's thinking and why he does certain things. Does he like you? What's up with his Jackie Chan obsession? What does he mean when he says he just wants to be friends? And what is up with that shaggy mass of hair on his head? (Word of advice: Don't mess with the hair. Boys are like Samson when it comes to their locks. Just like in that old Bible story, they have this bizarre idea that a haircut might strip them of their manly powers.)

Boyology delves into these and other mysteries of manhood, dissecting flirting tactics, offering dating suggestions, and providing tips on forming solid friendships with guys. It's an up-close-and-personal look at guys in their natural habitats, with profound analyses by teen girls (like you)—and boys themselves. Yes, we give guys a chance to tell their side of the story, and they make some surprising revelations about what love looks like from their points of view. You'll also get advice from a guy who's been there: my own hubby, Grant. Check out the "Grant on . . . " sections to get the dirt on everything from male flirting techniques to how you'll know if your guy deserves you (hint: it has a lot to do with respect). By the end of the book, you'll be well-versed in all things boy and ready to start some relationship studies of your own.

But before we dive into the nuts and bolts of boys, there's one incredibly important thing you need to know. . . .

YOU DON'T NEED A BOYFRIEND to feel good about yourself!

Say it with me now: *I DON'T NEED A BOYFRIEND.*

I only say this because, when I was in high school, there was one summer when I didn't date anyone. All my friends had boyfriends, and I was really worried I was missing out on something. Were they all having more fun than me? What did they have that I didn't? Was there something wrong with me?

In a word, *no*. I actually had more fun that summer than my friends with boyfriends did. While my BFF spent her summer vacation in California missing her guy, I totally enjoyed my family's trip to the Virgin Islands. No boyfriend would've been more fun than hanging out on a sandy beach and swimming with real-life sea turtles. And I didn't waste any of my time out of the water pining away for a boy at home.

Since then, there have been plenty of times when I didn't have a boyfriend and wasn't dating anyone special—and those have been some of the best times of my life. I've traveled all over the world, tried different jobs, and I absolutely loved the times I was single in college. Even though a boyfriend can be great, it's not necessary to have one in order to be happy or have a good time. I just wish I had known that during the summer before my junior year; I would've saved myself all those nights I went home and felt like crap.

So don't sweat it if you haven't found the right guy yet. You've got a great life going. And, in the meantime, you can start reading this book to get a top-tier guy education. Then, when Mr. Right (or Mr. Right Now) comes along, you'll be totally ready!

Happy reading!

Sarah

chapter 1

B-O-Y BASICS

Before we get into the befriending and dating of boys, we need to get to the bottom of the male mindset. And to do that, we need to ask the right questions.

When I asked the girls interviewed for this book what they wanted to know about guys in general, they had some killer questions (and I went straight to the source for some of the answers). Here are the bare essentials—things all girls need to know about boys:

Q+A

Q: "Do all guys forget to wash their hands, or is it just my brother?" —Ville, 14

A: "We almost always wash our hands, but not if we're in a big hurry or something. It's not the same for us. We get to stand to pee." —Marco, 17

Q: Why do guys treat girls differently when they're around their friends?" —Kaylee, 18

A: "Guys don't like all that lovey-dovey stuff, especially in front of their friends. But girls get all offended if we're not like hugging and kissing them all the time." —Landon, 16

Q: "What do guys talk about when girls aren't around?"—Anna, 16

A: "Mostly sports. Sometimes we talk about girls, but mostly sports and stuff." —Peter, 15

Q: "Why won't guys cry in front of girls?" —Sydney, 16

A: "It's not like we cry in front of guys either. We don't really cry in front of anyone." —Kevin, 16

Q: "Is a girl's appearance really more important than her personality?" —Lindsey, 15

A: "A cool personality is way more important than looks, but I think if you like someone's personality, you'll think she's attractive anyway." —Alan, 16

Q: "Why won't guys ever tell girls what they're thinking about? Instead, they just respond with things like 'nothing' or 'uhmmm, ahhh.'" —Jackie, 16

A: "My last girlfriend used to ask me what I was thinking about every ten minutes. Most of the time I wasn't thinking about anything, but she wouldn't believe me. I had to make up stuff to get her to stop asking." —Lance, 17

"[Guys] act like they like you, then they don't talk to you. Then if they do talk to you, they're like, 'Um, I kind of like your friend!' They're just strange people." —Emma Roberts, actress

"Boys frustrate me. I hate all their indirect messages. I hate game playing. Do you like me or don't you? Just tell me so I can get over you." —Kirsten Dunst, actress

"Boys are all weird. Every one of them is weird." —Mae Williams, actress

"Of all the animals, the boy is the most unmanageable." —Plato, Greek philosopher (probably the most famous of all these people)

Universally Boy

If scientists were going to construct a model of the modern guy, there are a few common characteristics they would have to include. For some reason, no matter what type of guy he is, almost every boy is guilty of the following:

- *The Head Nod* (Can't he just say "hi" like a normal person?)
- *The Farting* (Smelly)
- *The Burping* (Yuck)
- *The Way He Always Wants to Hug You When He's Super Sweaty* (Why does he think you would want to hug him after he just finished a rowdy game of touch football?)

Those habits can be pretty annoying, but they're generally manageable. (Note to self: Steer clear of sweaty guys post-workout.) What you really need to watch out for are the big gender differences, and here are seven of the biggest. Learn them well.

(Warning: A small percentage of guys will not fit all of these generalizations—but even if your guy doesn't fit all, chances are he has at least one of these traits.)

1. *Guys hate shopping.* Unless they're going to get a new baseball glove or Nintendo system, most boys walk into a store and turn into partial zombies, aimlessly wandering the aisles with a dull look in their eyes. That's because they're totally overwhelmed and probably don't care that lapis is the new shade this season. Save the shopping spree for a time when you aren't with lover boy.

Talk Isn't Cheap

"We can't read your minds or interpret girl talk, so just say what you mean and save us all the trouble." —Mike, 16

"Girls think that guys are tough, but deep down they can really hurt us, so they need to watch what they say." —Winston, 16

GRANT ON ...Shopping

I've gone on dates with girls who thought shopping would be a fun date activity. It is not. Let me repeat: It is not. Shopping is up there with teaching someone to drive a stick shift as one of the worst date activities in the world. That's another thing. A girl might think learning to drive stick in a guy's car is fun, but all the guy can think about is the smell of his burning clutch and the fact that he's about to throw up from all the jolting.

2. Guys are really defensive about their friends. Even if you think his buddy Ethan is a total punk, as long as he doesn't do wrong by you, leave it alone. Your boyfriend doesn't want to hear that you hate his friends. That's like bashing his family (another big no-no).

3. Guys don't notice all the flaws you see in yourself. Your big hips? Your chunky arms? That's all in your head! Really, it is. Unless you point out how your thighs rub together when you walk, he's not going to notice or care. Get over it! Have more confidence in yourself; confidence is one thing guys *do* notice. Someone who feels good about herself is way more fun to hang out with than someone who needs constant reassurance.

4. Guys are competitive—and not just about sports. With all that testosterone pumping through their veins, they're competitive about nearly everything. That's not necessarily a bad thing; a little competition never hurt anyone, and sometimes it can be really fun. Just make sure he's not too competitive with you. He should be happy about your success, just like you're happy for him when he aces a test or kicks butt in his hockey game.

5. Guys are just as puzzled by you as you are by them. Behind that sly grin, he's actually trying to figure out what to say next and wondering if you really

GUYS TELL IT LIKE IT IS:

Motivate Me!

"I want a girl who challenges me, rather than someone who's always my yes-woman. If she disagrees with me, I want her to argue! I'm looking for someone who makes me want to be a little better, a little smarter— someone who motivates me."
—Zach Gilford, actor

like him. So if he comes off as shy or a little dorky, go easy on him. He's as new to this whole girl–guy thing as you are.

6. Cocky guys are just self-conscious. Unfortunately, many
men have evolved to believe that acting cool will make them look cool. Whatever. If he's being cocky, remember that he's probably hiding his own major insecurities. You can probably relate a little (who doesn't feel insecure every so often?), but being unsure of himself isn't an excuse for being a jerk. Don't let him throw you off your game with his overly confident act. It's usually just that—an act.

7. Guys aren't into the plastic look. Ask around. You'll find
that most guys prefer natural looks over a lot of makeup and think a girl looks better in jeans and a T-shirt than a skimpy prom dress (not that they aren't drooling over you at prom). So let your natural beauty shine!

GRANT ON ... What Guys Really Think Is Cute

Sure, guys like cute girls. But every guy has a different definition of cute. Never think, "Guys would like me more if I were X type of girl." If you're confident and smart, you'll be much more interesting to guys than the girl who only talks about how much she's eaten that day. Every guy I know likes a girl who can actually carry on a conversation. And in case you didn't already know, asking a guy if you look fat is not carrying on a conversation. Guys hate that.

GUYS TELL IT LIKE IT IS:

Being Tough Enough

"Guys like feeling strong. I know it's a stereotype, but it's true."—**Jess, 17**

"Girls aren't the only ones who can feel nervous about being in a swimsuit. Guys are expected to look like Vin Diesel." —**Gabe, 18**

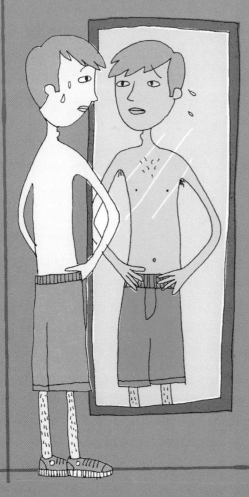

Keeping It Real

"I hate it when girls wear all that black stuff on their eyes. It looks like someone punched them in the face." —**Dustin, 15**

"I don't like fashion girls...the ones who care more about what you look like with them than who you are. It's like you're another part of their outfit." —**Greg, 18**

"I used to go out with girls only based on looks. Then I figured out those girls were really fake. Now I look for personality. I want someone I can actually stand to be around." —**Rob, 17**

"My girlfriend is gorgeous. Even after we play basketball together and she's all sweaty, she's beautiful. But she doesn't think she's pretty at all." —**Nick, 17**

"Wear less makeup and more clothes. Don't get me wrong, I like cleavage, but you should leave something to the imagination." —**Brian, 17**

EXTRA CREDIT

Are Girls and Guys Really That Different?

It depends. Sometimes you feel like you're on the same wavelength as him and other times he seems like a different species. But just because he likes Fall Out Boy doesn't necessarily mean there are scientific differences between you two . . . or does it? Here are a few random (and totally enlightening) facts to keep in the back of your mind the next time he does something that weirds you out. Maybe you can chalk some of those bizarre behaviors up to science.

- In her book *The Female Brain*, neuropsychiatrist Louann Brizendine says that women use 20,000 words per day and men use 7,000 words per day.

- But a 2007 Gallup poll showed that men talk to strangers more often than women do.

- The World Health Organization reports that guys are 2.7 times more likely than girls to be in a traffic accident.

- The World Health Organization also says that women have a 78 percent greater chance of becoming blind.

- One Brown University study showed that men have more water in their bodies than women—61 percent for the average guy compared to 52 percent for the average girl!

- On average, women are nearly 5 inches shorter than men!

Spamfo, a British company that studies all things related to spam (the e-mail kind, not the canned meat), says that a guy's computer is 21 percent more likely to get a computer virus than a girl's computer.

MR. PRESIDENT

THE TORTURED ARTIST

THE METROSEXUAL

THE HIP-HOPPER

TYPE SELECTOR
TURN TO THE TYPE OF YOUR CHOICE

MAMA'S BOY

THE TECH-TILIAN

THE SURF STUD

THE ATHLETICUS GREATIU

chapter 2

WHAT BREED IS YOUR BOYFRIEND?

Not to be confused with stereotypes, boy breeds are general boy classifications, meant to help you get a sense of the types of boys out there—and which one might be right for you. After all, it's much easier to understand one boy if you have a better sense of guys in general.

Bring On the Boys

The Tortured Artist

Celeb look-alike: John Mayer

In ten years, he'll be: Accepting an award for his artistic contribution to society

After school, you can find him: In his studio

His signature ringtone: Anything by Elliott Smith

Movie he has memorized: *Eternal Sunshine of the Spotless Mind*

His iPod is filled with: Underground music you haven't heard of

Dream car: No car for this cool cat—he prefers driving a vintage scooter

What he wears on a date: Dark jeans, a black T-shirt, and All-Stars

He never leaves the house without: His little notebook—who knows when genius will strike?

His ultimate date would be: Going to an art-house movie and talking at a coffee shop afterward

He looks up to: Stanley Kubrick

The Athleticus Greatius

Celeb look-alike: LeBron James

In ten years, he'll be: Playing fantasy sports with the other married guys around the office

After school, you can find him: On the field or court, obviously

His signature ringtone: Anything by Lenny Kravitz

Movie he has memorized: *Hoosiers*

His iPod is filled with: Get-pumped songs by Van Halen and Journey

Dream car: A big manly SUV

What he wears on a date: His championship ring

He never leaves the house without: His lucky baseball cap

His ultimate date would be: The Super Bowl

He looks up to: Peyton Manning

The Metrosexual

Celeb look-alike: Orlando Bloom

In ten years, he'll be: Working as a graphic designer

After school, you can find him: Shopping (he's the best guy to hit the mall with)

His signature ringtone: Anything by Justin Timberlake

Movie he has memorized: *Oceans 11* . . . and *12* . . . and *13*

His iPod is filled with: A mix of '70s rock, '80s hair bands, and other songs they play over and over on the radio

Dream car: VW Jetta

What he wears on a date: Jeans and a designer-logo T-shirt

He never leaves the house without: His hair gel

His ultimate date would be: Sushi at the hottest new restaurant

He looks up to: Ryan Seacrest

Mr. President

Celeb look-alike: Toby Maguire

In ten years, he'll be: Running a country, or at least a company

After school, you can find him: Volunteering— he has to beef up that resume if he's going to get into Yale

His signature ringtone: "Hail to the Chief"

Movie he has memorized: *Independence Day*

His iPod is filled with: Anything by Coldplay

Dream car: Mercedes-Benz S-Class Sedan

What he wears on a date: A navy blazer and red tie

He never leaves the house without: Looking in the mirror and giving himself a winning smile

His ultimate date would be: A swanky dinner and tickets to the opera

He looks up to: JFK

The Mama's Boy

Celeb look-alike: Justin Timberlake

In ten years, he'll be: A bachelor—no girl will be able to live up to Mom

After school, you can find him: At home, scarfing down oatmeal cookies—no one makes them like Mom

His signature ringtone: Anything by Billy Joel

Movie he has memorized: *Titanic*

His iPod is filled with: Songs you hear as you're skipping over the soft-rock station

Dream car: Volvo hatchback

What he wears on a date: The V-neck sweater Mom got him for his birthday

He never leaves the house without: His cell phone, so he can call home

His ultimate date would be: Doubles tennis, with his parents

He looks up to: His mother (duh)

The Surf Stud

Celeb look-alike: Zac Efron

In ten years, he'll be: Living near the ocean or ski slopes

After school, you can find him: Skateboarding with his posse

His signature ringtone: "California," by Phantom Planet

Movie he has memorized: *Old School*

His iPod is filled with: Bob Marley

Dream car: Jeep Wrangler

What he wears on a date: Shorts, a polo shirt, and flip-flops

He never leaves the house without: His sunglasses

His ultimate date would be: A bonfire on the beach with a midnight swim in the ocean

He looks up to: Kelly Slater—he's made a career out of chilling on the beach

The Tech-tilian

Celeb look-alike: Michael Cera

In ten years, he'll be: Famous for designing a new brand of computer

After school, you can find him: On his home computer

His signature ringtone: Anything by Radiohead

Movie he has memorized: *Monty Python and the Holy Grail*

His iPod is filled with: Uber-techno British bands he discovered online

Dream car: A hybrid

What he wears on a date: Tennis shoes and a button-up

He never leaves the house without: His iPhone. Does he think he's going to miss an important e-mail?

His ultimate date would be: Comic-Con

He looks up to: Steve Jobs

The Hip-Hopper

Celeb look-alike: Lupe Fiasco

In ten years, he'll be: Running a record label

After school, you can find him: Playing basketball with his boys

His signature ringtone: Nas's latest hit

Movie he has memorized: *Hustle & Flow*

His iPod is filled with: Rap and hip-hop, of course

Dream car: A pimped-out Denali

What he wears on a date: Anything with a little bling

He never leaves the house without: His headphones

His ultimate date would be: Front-row tickets to a Lakers game

He looks up to: Kanye West

"I'm really, really picky. [My ideal guy is] someone who has their you-know-what together. There is nothing less attractive than a guy who is a jerk and has an ego." —Amanda Bynes, actress

"I am an equal-opportunity dater. . . . I have no type. I'm all over the map." —Mandy Moore, actress/singer

Maroon 5 singer, **Adam Levine**, is proud of being a Mama's Boy! *"Have you ever noticed that guys who have good relationships with their mothers know how to behave? I'm a mama's boy—that's why I'm nice."*

Actress **Ali Larter** knows her type! *"I hate pretty-looking boys. I'd rather have a guy with a potbelly than one who's in the gym all the time and watches what he eats."*

"All I need is for him to be funny and someone I can have a conversation with." —Kelly Clarkson, singer

Which Boy Breed Is Best for You?

First, figure out what you most want in a relationship. Then, keep reading to get some general information on which boy breed is most likely to be your type, based on what you want. Don't worry if you find yourself liking multiple "types" of guys. It's all about experimentation and figuring out what works for you!

IF YOU LIKE . . .

Romance: Go for the Tortured Artist. He's the kind of guy who will write you poetry and take you for long, wistful walks under the stars. And since he's the perfect mix of intellectually sexy and geeky-cute, you won't have any trouble staring into his eyes when he starts reciting, "How do I love thee . . . "

Action and Adventure: The Athleticus Greatius has energy to spare. And, with all of his athletic ability, he enjoys taking things to the limit; there's never a dull moment with this cutie!

Sophistication and Style: The Metrosexual is the guy for you. He's a mix of culture and panache; he's the kind of guy who knows about all the hot new restaurants and goings-on around town, long before they become mainstream.

Success and Straight A's: You'll probably be attracted to a Mr. President. A future business tycoon or politician, this guy is a charmer and commands attention when he walks into a room. Just be sure you don't become a trophy on his arm. You have a lot to offer, too!

Chivalry: The Mama's Boy is one guy who knows how to treat a woman with tenderness. Just watch how much he respects his mom, and you'll see that he's the kind of guy who will open the car door for you and pull out your chair at dinner.

Chilling Out: Take in the sunset with the Surf Stud—he's the quintessential easygoing guy. He's someone you'll feel comfortable opening up to, since his laid-back attitude is perfect for listening.

Latest and Greatest Gadgets: Find yourself a Tech-tilian. Super smart—sometimes too smart for his own good—this guy might not be super-stylish, but he'll never run out of things to talk about because he knows so many interesting things. This is the guy you'd want to get stuck in an elevator with. He'd be rational and you'd be anything but bored!

Bad Boys: The Hip-Hopper is the ultimate bad boy—but deep down he's all sweetheart. Just make sure the macho lyrics of his beloved hip-hop don't convince him to treat you badly.

EXTRA CREDIT — Dreaming Up Your McDreamy

What if your boy doesn't belong to any of these breeds, or you like a combination of them? You might have discovered a new breed—or a hybrid!

ONE REALLY COOL GIRL interviewed for this book, Ashley, has an ongoing list in her journal called "My Next Boyfriend Will Be . . . " I never wrote an actual list when I was in high school, but I knew I wanted a guy who could carry on good conversation, who listened to old-school rock, and was lean but built. I ended up finding him in college—totally worth the wait.

Don't be afraid to dream big, like Ashley, and make your own next-boyfriend list. Just remember that it's a work in progress—don't ditch a guy just because he likes red Popsicles better than purple ones. Opposites do attract, after all.

Here are a few ideas to help you get your own list started, whether you put it in your journal or on your blog. Add traits or adjust these entries according to what kind of guy you want. And be sure to keep it somewhere easy to access, so you can make sure the guys you're dating are living up to your dreams!

MY NEXT BOYFRIEND WILL . . .

1. Look like _____
2. Take me on a date in which we _____
3. Think my _____ is my best feature
4. Have a great _____
5. Like to _____ in his spare time
6. Have the following qualities: _____
7. Listen to _____ on his iPod
8. Read books such as _____
9. Know how to _____
10. Love _____ about me

chapter 3

I ♥ YOU: When You're Head-Over-Heels in Like

You've finally met that one-in-a-mil guy. He's smart, sexy, and every time he turns around and meets your eyes during chem class your heart practically stops and you realize you're holding your breath. He's definitely the guy for you. Only he doesn't know it yet.

In the animal kingdom, flirting is an intricate dance— sometimes literally. The male rainbow lorikeet (a really colorful parakeet), woos his mate with a series of wobbly steps that resemble footwork from *Saturday Night Fever*. As soon as he sees a potential girlfriend, he busts a move. If the female bird is into it, she'll nuzzle up against him and let him smooth her feathers. If she's not interested, she moves on and he finds someone else to flirt with.

It's the same thing with you. You're dancing around your feelings, opening up a little but not completely, and testing the waters with the other bird. If he's interested, he might let you smooth his feathers. And if not, at least you know so you can move on to a different, worthier dance partner.

Get Your Flirt On

Since bird-mating moves aren't likely to work on McDreamy, you'll need some other ways to let the flirting fly. And as with all things, some ways are better than others. Here are a few good and bad ways to perfect your "dance."

Bad: Making eye contact by staring at him.
Good: Catching his eye and holding his glance just a little longer than usual. Then giving him a little smile.

The key to eye flirting is keeping it light. If you look *too* long at a guy, it will seem like you're either staring him down or acting stalker-ish. Neither is good. Just a quick glance (with the essential grin) is flirting—without even saying a word!

· · ·

Bad: Laughing at every word that comes out of his mouth. You want him to know you like his jokes, right?
Good: Laughing when you think he says something funny.

Laughing hysterically every time your crush says something is a surefire way to come across as insincere. Fake laughter is as transparent as clear lip gloss: he'll be able to tell that you don't mean it. Instead, smile at him when you think he's being cute, and when he says something funny feel free to give him a wholehearted, utterly sincere giggle.

Bad: Hanging on him every time you're together. You have to touch him to show you're interested.

Good: Occasionally brushing up against his shoulder or touching his arm.

In flirting, a little contact goes a long way. You want to show your crush that you're into him and get a sense of how he feels about you. Does he smile back when you flash your pearly whites? Does he step closer to you when you whisper something? Draping yourself all over him does not constitute flirting because you really won't be able to gauge his feelings if you're suffocating him. Instead, stay cool and keep it playful—flirting is meant to be fun!

• • •

Bad: Gushing over every little detail, like his sweater, hat, jeans, shoes, socks—you get the picture.

Good: Complimenting him on something specific, like his new iPod. You love the green color.

Guys love a little flattery (who doesn't?), but keep it sincere if you want to make an impression. Going overboard and complimenting every little thing about him makes it sound like you're putting him on a pedestal, which can be totally overwhelming. Focus on one or two things you really like about him. Considering he's your crush, you shouldn't have a hard time finding something!

Of course, those are just the basics. Here are six other tried-and-true ways to show him that you want to be more than just friends.

1. Find out what you have in common. If he spends time after school at the gym and you're a total yoga buff, suggest you start working out together. Hanging out in the same places and doing things you both enjoy will give you more time to get to know each other.

2. Start a real conversation by asking him a semi-personal question. Not about something he'd only share in therapy, mind you, but something to get him talking about his interests and what he likes to do. A basic question that requires more than a "yes" or "no" answer, like "What did you do last weekend?" is a good way to get things rolling.

3. Stand closer to him than you have to. Not so close that you're going to lose your balance and fall over, but close enough that he can feel you there. Believe me, he'll notice!

4. Do something spontaneous (but not crazy). Did it just snow? Suggest you go make snow angels. Is it superhot? What about taking a run through the school sprinklers? Guys love it when girls are willing to try new, silly things.

GRANT ON ... Spontaneity

I loved dating girls who were up for anything. When Sarah and I were first dating, we were on a hike and I convinced her to go swimming underneath a waterfall. The waterfall was actually runoff from a glacier, and the water was so cold you couldn't breathe. There were tons of people around, but no one would dare get in the water. I waded in and, after feeling how cold it was, told her she didn't have to do it, but she dove in headfirst anyway, and I had newfound respect for her. None of the other girls I'd gone out with would've ever had the guts to jump in.

5. Be a good friend. By being there if he needs to talk or wants a study buddy, you're showing him that you really care. Just remember not to forfeit your own life for his. You don't want to be the kind of person who is always hanging around, like a third wheel.

6. The good ole music mix.

Make him an iPod mix or burn a CD with some of your favorite songs. As DJ AM says, "The best way to get closer to a guy you have a crush on is to have a music-listening session together."

GUYS TELL IT LIKE IT IS:

It's All about the Little Things

"I love it when a girl wears my baseball hat." —Zach, 16

"Any girl I go out with has to like my dog." —Carter, 16

Taking Matters into Your Own Hands: How to Ask Him Out

After two months of flirting during physics class, you can barely take it anymore. Why can't your lab partner just man up and ask you out?! Sometimes guys are too shy to get up the nerve to call and ask if you want to hang out on Friday night (like it's that hard). You might have to be the one to take the plunge.

Some girls don't think it's cool to be the one doing the asking, but remember that we aren't living in the early 1900s anymore. Our feminist sisters didn't fight for our rights for nothing! So unless you are seriously opposed to women asking men out, take a deep breath and make the call. It's not like you're asking him to spend the rest of his life with you. It's just one night. And if you're super nervous about letting him know you're into him, ask him to come hang out with a few people. Remember, there's safety in numbers.

GIRL TALK: Would You Ask Him Out?

"If you're a girl, and you're brave and confident enough to ask a guy out, I say GO FOR IT!" —Lindsay, 14

"I used to wait for guys to make the first move, but now I've found it's better to just do it myself so I won't have to sit around waiting and playing games." —Lyndie, 17

"[The issue of] asking guys out is one of those things that makes me an embarrassment to the feminist movement. I never ask [guys] out on dates. I think the guy should make the first move. Otherwise, what is he? Shy? A pushover?" —Heather, 16

"I don't ask guys out on dates. I try to give enough hints, gestures, and contact to let them know that I'm interested, and then they pick it up from there." —Jessi, 15

When *Teen* magazine asked JJ from NLT how he'd feel if a girl asked him out, he said, "I think it would be absolutely adorable because it shows that she really likes me and doesn't care what other people think." What a guy!

How to Ask Him Out Without Actually Asking

You know you like him, and you think he feels the same way. At some point, someone's going to have to make a move. Here are a few ways to suggest that the two of you get together without spelling out the fact that you're dying to go on a date with him.

1. Pick up some movie passes and, the next day at school, pull them out of your bag while he's around. Mention that you're dying to see the latest Jessica Alba flick. Maybe he'd be interested in tagging along?

2. You're going to a party and want to make sure he's going to be there. A simple text saying you'll look for him that night says it all.

3. Bump (yes, literally) into him before lunch and say you're running out to grab a bagel. You'd love some company. (What guy can turn down food?)

When He Won't Take the Bait

You've tried everything and still can't seem to get through to the guy? Either he's going blind (in which case you'll have to rely on your melodious voice and passionate conversational skills to win him over), or, more likely, he's "just not that into you." Harsh. But you don't want to waste your flirting finesse on someone who's not interested. Here are a few telltale signs that it's time to move on:

He blows you off on a regular basis. Whether he forgets to call you back, doesn't return your e-mails, or flakes out on Saturday night plans, if he's not participating in the communication, it probably means he doesn't care to communicate at all.

He tells you what a great friend you are. By emphasizing your "friend" status, he's saying he doesn't want to take things to the next level.

You see him flirting with other girls. While this might not necessarily be meant to hurt you, it's a definite sign his heart is somewhere else.

SHE'S BEEN THERE

"*I really liked this guy, and for a while I thought he liked me back. We talked a lot and kind of flirted in class, but every time I asked him to do something, he already had other plans. Then one night I asked him to go to this party with me, and he said he had a family dinner. I skipped the party since I didn't have a date and went to a movie with my mom. Guess who was there on a date with another girl? I just wish he wouldn't have led me on if he liked someone else.*" —Cassie, 17

Clandestine Crushing

Part of the fun of crushing on someone is talking about it, but remember to be discreet and refrain from posting all your feelings on MySpace. Telling the whole school you're in love with your lab partner could get embarrassing, both for you and the guy. It might be cute at first—what guy doesn't like being the object of someone's affection? But after a while, it will just get annoying and seem really immature. (And you don't want your former feelings following you around forever once you've started crushing on someone else.) Instead of blabbering about him to everyone, just keep it between a few good friends—but feel free to gush to them all you want!

GRANT ON ... Flirting

The first phase of flirting is eye contact, whether you're twelve or twenty. It's tough being a guy because you're always afraid of putting yourself out there. You don't want to be rejected. That's why girls have to step up a little. If he's giving you sidelong glances, he's into you, but he's trying to play it cool. If you're interested, smile back or something, so he knows he's not about to look like an idiot when he comes up to talk to you.

Making His Move

Suppose you're just minding your own business, and a guy you know starts treating you a little differently. What's the deal? Is he giving you the puzzled look because he's wondering what you're thinking, or because you have something stuck in your teeth? When he says "hi" in the hall, is he just being nice, or is he seeking you out? With all the mixed signals guys put out there, how are you supposed to know if he's hitting on you or just being weird? Here are some signals that are not at all mixed.

He gives you a playful nudge or poke in the side. This is basically left over from his days on the playground when he used to punch girls if he liked them. By finding a way to touch you, he's showing he's interested, but he's doing it in a way that doesn't put him at risk for getting rejected.

He wants to help out. If he's willing to volunteer with you on a Saturday morning or help you study, there's a good chance he's head over heels. Not only is he offering up his free time, but he wants to feel like he's doing something to deserve you. Such a guy move!

He offers you a ride home. This is a roundabout way of saying he wants to be alone with you and at the same time wants to make sure you get home safely. So cute!

He gives you a nickname. He might as well come right out and say he's into you, because coming up with a "pet" name, even if it is a joke, shows that he's been thinking about you and thinks you deserve some special treatment.

He does something to impress you. Whether it's winning a basketball game or telling you he aced his physics test, he wants you to see what a hot commodity he is. And as Madison, 17, says, "I like guys that try to impress me. I think it's kinda sexy."

Ttl Flrt

Texting and IMs will never replace good old-fashioned face-to-face flirting, but they can be a great way to get things going, especially if you get tongue-tied when you chat with a total cutie. Not only is texting super convenient, but it gives you a little breathing room to gauge how he feels. A 2007 Associated Press/AOL poll shows that 43 percent of teenagers IM things they wouldn't say in person. Hmmm. I wonder what they're saying!

A Few Things to Remember About Text Flirting

Keep it short and simple. Any message that's going to be longer than two screens is too long for a text. Not only can it get annoying to flip through the message, but guys can have short attention spans. If you have lots to say, just make the call.

Don't send text after text after text. Text messages should be a short version of a conversation, so let him reply before sending another one. You don't want to be the only one having the conversation.

Sometimes text flirting gets lost in translation. Before you flip out because he sends you a "c u" message, make sure you know exactly what he means. He probably isn't breaking up with you; he's just turning his phone off for class.

"I do a lot of text messaging. It's easy to flirt with girls via text. You throw the little X's, the little smiley faces. . . . But if the texts continue for more than three or four trades, you've got to make the phone call." —Chris Evans, actor

EXTRA CREDIT

Quiz: What's Your Flirt Style?

Answer *yes* or *no* to the following questions to figure out what kind of flirt you are!

1. When you see a cute guy at a party, you go over and start a conversation with him.

2. You ask guys out more often than they ask you out.

3. You have more guy friends than girl friends on MySpace.

4. You're pretty sure the guy you like knows it.

5. If your friend sees a hot guy at a concert, you're the one who asks for his number.

6. You kiss every guy you go out with.

7. Your friends get jealous because you get all the guys.

8. You check your crush's MySpace page every day, if not every hour.

9. You know all of your crush's friends.

10. More than one person has called you a "total flirt."

Scoring:

If you answered YES *to all 10 questions, you are a* CONFIDENT CHICK.
If you see something you want, you aren't afraid to go for it. Most of
the time, that's one of your best qualities, but sometimes you come
across as too confident and too much of a flirt. It doesn't hurt to
leave some things to the imagination. So next time a guy asks what
you're thinking about, don't say "you"—even if you can't get your
mind off of him. Keep him on his toes!

If you answered YES *to 5–9 questions, you are a* SELECTIVE SWEETIE.
You are the perfect balance of flirty and friendly. You don't try too
hard to be sexy, and you don't spend all your time thinking about
guys. (But you are willing to make the first move if he isn't taking
the hint.) Your mix of flash and modesty is one of the reasons guys
think you're so hot!

If you answered YES *to fewer than 5 questions, you are a* BASHFUL BABE.
There's nothing wrong with shying away from flirting if there's no
one you're interested in, but make sure you aren't avoiding it just to
save yourself from getting hurt! Love and relationships are risky, but
they're totally worth it. Don't be afraid to put yourself on the line
once in a while! Let loose a little. Flirting is meant to be fun!

chapter 4

THE FIRSTS OF FIRST DATES:
And the Rest of the Dating Game

This is how the dictionary defines dating:

The act in which two people, most often a male and female, spend time together with the intention of getting to know each other in order to find a mate

This is how you define dating:

1: When a guy you like asks you to join him in an activity that requires some planning, thought, and romance; **2:** When you ask a guy you're interested in to be your companion for a specific activity, whether alone or with a group

And this is how he defines dating:

A very rare occurrence, usually a school dance, that is made official by his wearing a tie and having to make a dinner reservation

• • •

That's a pretty broad spectrum of definitions. So how do you know when the date is really a date in his mind? It's actually easier than you think. Just check for one of these four telltale signs.

1. *He specifically seeks you out* so he can ask you to do something. It could be a phone call, an IM, a text, or an in-person conversation, but if he gets your attention and flat-out asks if you're free on Friday, consider it a real date.

2. *He asks you weeks in advance.* If he's planning further out than the coming weekend, he's been thinking really hard about locking you in. Total date.

3. *He shows up at your door with flowers.* It's simple: For most guys, flowers equal planning, and planning equals date. Whether it's a bouquet of roses or a single carnation, if he brings you anything in bloom, it's a date.

4. *He wears a suit,* a tux, or even just a button-down shirt and nice jeans. Dressing up isn't something most guys relish, so if he's pressed and polished, you're going on a date.

GRANT ON ... Guys and Dating

I don't think the word *dating* was in my vocabulary in high school. Aside from school dances, it was more about hanging out with a group and trying to work in some alone time. At most, I would say I was "going out" with someone—a guy's noncommittal way of saying someone is your girlfriend without actually using the G-word—and even that was pretty rare. It seemed to me that girls were the ones who usually wanted a boyfriend, not the other way around.

Playing One-on-One

A little bit like one-on-one basketball, one-on-one dates have a whole different feel than group activities. For starters, it's just you and Mr. Hottie—you can't count on your BFF to bail you out of an awkward silence, and he doesn't have his friends to distract him from your clever conversation and winning smile. Even though you've been dying for some alone time with your dream guy, the one-on-one date can be a little intimi-dating. How can you make a date feel as comfortable as when you're hanging out with friends?

CELEB SHOUT-OUT!

"I would never take a girl on a first date to dinner and a movie, ever! It's got to be something active and random. Like the last first date I went on, I took the girl go-karting. That way, you don't have to sit at a table and stare at each other. It takes the pressure off because you're doing something fun."
—*Zach Gilford, actor*

Dating Isn't Totally Dead

Contrary to popular belief—and your own experiences with wussy guys—people are pairing off more than you might think. According to Mediamark Research, 57 percent of teens say they regularly go on dates. Now, if only you could find those guys who took part in the survey . . .

First-Date Don'ts

First dates—like first kisses, your first time behind the steering wheel, and every other type of first—should be exciting, but they often end up being overwhelming and stressful. You want everything to be perfect, but how can you plan for something you've never actually experienced? If you want to make it to the second date, be sure to avoid these four first-date don'ts.

1. *If you really want to get to know him, don't go to a movie* on your first date. You can't talk at all, and there's always that pressure of whether you should hold hands. Not to mention that even a fast-paced car-racing scene can't take your mind off the fact that he still hasn't put his arm around you. Of course, there's the opposite school of thought that says movies can trigger some good conversation during a post-film ice cream run. If you're the type that needs a little conversational inspiration, a movie might be your ticket to date heaven.

2. *Don't mention old boyfriends* or other dates you've been on. No guy wants to feel like he's trying to live up to someone else. Imagine how you would feel if you had to spend all night hearing about how amazing his last girlfriend was!

3. Aside from a quick "hello" at the door, *don't force him to do the whole meet-the-fam thing;* it's too much pressure for someone you're going out with for the first time. Don't worry if your

Dating by IM?

An Associated Press/AOL poll found that 22 percent of teens use IM to ask people out or accept a date. That's a good way to cover up that little scream of excitement when he finally asks you out. With an IM, he won't hear it at all!

dad insists on meeting a guy before you're allowed out of the house. That's totally normal, and most guys will probably expect it. It's just the dragged-out introductions that are killer.

4. Iron out plans beforehand, so you don't show up in a cocktail dress for a night of sledding. You might look hot, but you won't have much fun and will probably feel super self-conscious the whole time.

Date-Night Prep

Set the Mood: Make a Date-Night Music Mix

You've got your going-out mix for getting pumped up before Girls' Night Out, and you have your mellow-ish tunes that you turn on when you're getting ready for bed. So why not make a date-night mix? Not only can music totally set the mood, whether you want the mood to be fun or romantic, but it can also provide something to talk about when you and McDreamy run out of things to say about your English teacher or favorite football team. Hey, before you're his girlfriend, you're bound need to some conversational inspiration!

But one important thing to remember when making a date-night mix is not to choose all girlie music—you know, a Madonna and "Girls Just Want to Have Fun" compilation. Not many guys dig Mandy Moore, although "Candy" is a GNO classic. The lists below will give you some ideas for boy-friendly music that you'll like, too. And these aren't the only songs that will work. Just scroll through your own MP3 player for even more ideas.

The I–Want–a–Kiss–at–the–End–of–the–Night Romance Mix:

1. "No Woman, No Cry," by the Fugees
2. "Blue Moon Revisited," by the Cowboy Junkies
3. "Love Is All Around," by the Troggs
4. "Wish You Were Here," by Pink Floyd
5. "Fade Into You," by Mazzy Star
6. "Sleep," by Azure Ray
7. "Bandstand in the Sky," by Pete Yorn
8. "Come Away with Me," by Norah Jones
9. "Fields of Gold," by Sting
10. "With or Without You," by U2

The Time–of–Your–Life Fun Mix:

1. "Satisfaction," by the Rolling Stones
2. "Sexy Back," by Justin Timberlake
3. "Island in the Sun," by Weezer
4. "Suddenly I See," by KT Tunstall
5. "Heavy Metal Drummer," by Wilco
6. "Girlfriend," by Avril Lavigne
7. "Girls Own Love," by Andrew W. K.
8. "Words and Guitar," by Sleater-Kinney

9. "Dreaming," by Blondie

10. "(I've Had) The Time of My Life," from the *Dirty Dancing* soundtrack (Duh! You have to include this one in a time-of-your-life mix!)

The Getting-to-Know-You Conversation-Starter Mix:

1. "Let It Be," by the Beatles
2. "Never Know," by Jack Johnson
3. "Girlfriend in a Coma," by the Smiths
4. "On the Radio," by Regina Spektor
5. "Me Gustas Tú," by Manu Chao
6. "I Turn My Camera On," by Spoon
7. "Fit but You Know It," by the Streets
8. "Dry the Rain," by the Beta Band
9. "Oh! Sweet Nuthin'," by the Velvet Underground
10. "Let Forever Be," by the Chemical Brothers

Conversation Counts

Of course, you can't rely solely on the stereo to create conversational harmony. You'll have to actually talk, too. It might sound a little old-fashioned, but good conversation is the key to a good time. Seriously. You know those weird moments of silence that feel like hours but are actually just a few seconds? You want to avoid those at ALL COSTS! But solid conversation doesn't involve blabbering like an idiot. Get him talking about himself, preferably on a topic you'll enjoy too, and you won't have to worry about awkward pauses. For example, if you know he has a German shepherd and you love dogs, ask him how long he's had a pet. Or, if he seems to go on a lot of family trips and you love to travel, ask him about the last vacation he took. You get the idea. You'll also find out if you two have anything in common, besides the fact that you're totally hot for each other.

As you're talking, take notice of whether your crush stops to ask you any questions about your interests and life. If he can't stop talking about how much he can bench-press or he won't stop reciting lines from *Austin Powers*, you'll probably want to think twice before getting serious. How long can you actually listen to stories about him, and only him? Plus, a good date will actually care what you have to say, and that's what makes for really good banter.

GIRL (AND GUY) TALK: Conversation = Connection

"My favorite date was when I went out with this girl, and we ended up talking in the car for like an hour. She ended up being my girlfriend." —Seth, 17

"Conversation is the key to my heart." —Maddy, 18

Awkward Is as Awkward Does

No matter how amazing a conversationalist you are, you may still have a few uncomfortable moments on dates. But don't worry. Most of the time, the guy will be just as nervous as you are! Take it from Daniel Radcliffe (a.k.a. Harry Potter), "I'm getting better now, but I used to be incredibly awkward with girls. . . . Any guy who says 'I've never had an awkward moment with a girl' is a liar."

Activity Matters, Too

Even if you've mastered the art of conversation, you'll need to actually do something on the date. Having a plan (even if he doesn't) can help keep things interesting for both of you. Sometimes your guy might need a little help in the planning department.

Note to reader: High school guys are sometimes lacking in date creativity. So when he asks what you want to do, have some (realistic) ideas ready. (No, flying to Paris for the night is NOT realistic.)

Four Date-tastic Plans You Can Always Fall Back On

1. **Bake-it-up.** Sometimes all you need for a good date is a little sugar (and a few other ingredients). Pull out your favorite recipe, and bake a treat! You can eat it all yourselves, take some around to a few friends, or he can win over your mom with a plate of homemade goodness. He is SO delicious!

2. Do-gooding. Volunteer at a local food bank or homeless shelter for a night, and spend some time making a real difference in the world. Plus, who wouldn't like a guy who's willing to spend his free time helping out those in need?

3. Check out your high school sports teams. The girls' volleyball team might be awesome, but you'll never know unless you see a game. Plus, a little school spirit can be cute.

4. Dinner and a movie. This is a classic date for a reason. Just make sure he doesn't pick *A Nightmare on Elm Street 17* as the movie, unless you want to pee your pants in front of him.

BRING CHIVALRY BACK

How many times have you gone out with a guy, and he's forgotten to open the door for you? Or left you to pull out your own chair? It's not that you're helpless—you can definitely sit yourself down at a dinner table—but it would be nice if he could show you some respect. These days, chivalry has nearly lost its meaning—and its appeal. But we can bring it back to life by (nicely) demanding some respect.

Katherine, 16, did just that. She'd been dating a guy for a few weeks, and he'd been really great so far. On this day, they were planning to go on a casual hike in the mountains nearby. She was hanging out in the kitchen waiting for him to ring the doorbell, when she heard some honking. "He would never just honk for me," she thought, and stayed put. Less than two minutes later, more honking.

Curious, she got up and looked out her front window. Sitting there, in his mom's Jeep, was her date, honking for her to come out. Katherine is no princess, but she knew if she went out, that would be it: the end of doorbell-ringing date pickups. So she pulled a chair up to the window and waited. He actually went through two more honking sessions before he realized she wasn't coming, got out of his car, and walked up to the front door.

When she opened up the door, Katherine said, "I wondered how long it would take you to figure out I don't respond to honking." Then she gave him a kiss on the cheek and walked out of the house. She didn't start a fight, but she did make her point. He never honked for her again.

GIRL TALK:

The Definition of a Great Date

According to **Avery, 16**, "A great date is when you discover that you click." Amen, sister!

Check, Please

Since the dawn of dating, it's been tradition that the guy pays for dinner—but now that's starting to change. These days, girls pick up the check as often, if not more, than guys. Sometimes that's fair, but you shouldn't always be footing the bill. So how do you know who should pay?

Here's the rule to live by:
Whoever does the asking does the paying.

For example, if he calls and asks if you're free for a movie, you are totally right to expect that he'll buy the tickets. But if you're the one who wants to see the latest *Mission Impossible* and you ask him to come along, it's a nice gesture to pay his way.

The same goes for school dances. If he asks you to prom, he should pay for the basics—the tickets, dinner, pictures, and your corsage. (You have to buy a dress, after all!) But if he wants to splurge on extras, like a limo, you should offer to share some of the cost. No one wants to go bust for a dance! If the dance is girls' choice, and you ask him out, you should plan on bringing cash to cover the night.

Of course, if you're just hanging out as a group, you might go Dutch. No, we aren't talking about a trip to Holland. It's old-school lingo for both people paying their own way, and it's a good idea if you're eating out or seeing a movie with a bunch of people. That way, there's no awkward moment when you're splitting the bill and someone unexpectedly has to pay for someone else.

But what if you end up going Dutch or paying his way every time you go out?

If your date lets you pay for everything, he's taking advantage of you—and you deserve better than that! Relationships are meant to be partnerships: You each have to give a little. If he can't afford to treat you to dinner every once in a while, then he needs to get creative and find less expensive activities, or get a job! And remember that paying is definitely a two-way street. If you want to be treated, you also need to treat, so make sure you pick up the check every once in a while, too.

Another Good Reason to Carry That Cute Clutch

When Alison's mom handed her some cash before she left for prom and told her it was always good to be prepared, Alison thought she was just being paranoid. Everyone knew Greg was the most pulled-together guy in her class. There's no way he would leave her out in the cold or make her pay for dinner! So she was shocked when the check came, and Greg started shuffling through his pockets. Then, without saying anything, he got up and bolted for the front of the restaurant. Alison panicked. Was he ditching her with the bill?

Actually, no. In a totally weird turn of events, someone had mistaken Greg's coat for his and left the restaurant with it. Which wouldn't have been that big of a deal, but Greg had accidentally left his wallet in his coat pocket. And since his coat was gone, his wallet—and all his money—was, too.

Luckily, Alison had those bills from her mom so she was able to cover dinner. Greg was totally embarrassed (and he paid her back a few days later), but because she had some money with her, their date wasn't ruined. Leave it to the girl to save the date!

To Kiss or Not to Kiss

You got the guy. You've had the date. And now it's time to say "good night." Will there be a quick hug at the door, a polite peck on the cheek, or will the two of you seal the deal with a kiss?

The answer is: It's up to you. Do what feels comfortable, and don't let him pressure you into doing something you're not ready to do. If you want to a little kissing action, then go ahead and make your move—bat those mascara-pumped lashes and pucker up, buttercup. Waiting for him to take the first step? Pay attention to his signals: Is he leaning in? Holding eye contact a little longer than necessary? Talking more softly than normal so you have to get close to hear him? Giving you a shy smile? If yes, he's probably working up the courage to kiss you. And if you're into it, why not meet him halfway? But if it doesn't seem like tonight's the night, let it go. Casually take a step back, flash those pearly whites, and thank him for a good time. If things continue to go well between the two of you, you'll get there when you're both ready.

I WANNA HOLD YOUR HAND

A lot of girls prefer to wait until the third (or fourth or fifth) date to seal the deal with a smooch. And they aren't the only ones. Actress Lauren Conrad says, "I don't kiss on the first date. My friends always make fun of me for that! But I will hold hands. . . . If a guy's not gonna hold your hand, do you really want to kiss him?"

Seven Steps to Becoming an Awesome Kisser

1. Go with the moment. Are you holding hands? Gazing into each other's eyes? Romance is the key to a good kiss.

2. Meet him halfway. Lean in close to his face, and if he moves toward you, he's thinking the same thing. Now the gap between you is closed, and you're ready to seal the deal.

3. Close your eyes. Not totally necessary, but it can be weird (and distracting) to be looking at each other when you're that close. Closing your eyes lets you stay completely in the moment.

4. Touch your lips to his. Keep your lips partially open, and don't squeeze them together while you kiss—even though that's how you make a kissy face—because it makes your lips hard and pointy.

5. Apply pressure. Don't press too hard, just enough so you can actually feel his lips pressing against yours.

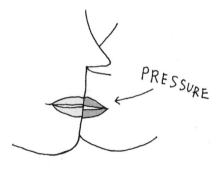

6. Optional: If you're getting into it, wrap your arms around his neck. It's an extra level of closeness.

7. Pull away slowly. You don't want to break the momentum of the moment, so keep all your movements slow and steady. Think of a slow-motion sequence in a movie, speeding it up just a little bit.

Advanced Kissing

After you've perfected the basic kiss, you can expand your horizons with more complex smooching techniques.

The Tongue Twister: Often called a French kiss, the tongue twister is one of the messier kisses. You and your boyfriend basically move your tongues around in each other's mouths. To prevent this kiss from feeling like you have a snake slithering over your teeth, keep everything soft and slow. *Steaminess Factor: B*

The Open–Mouthed Kiss: This is kind of like a French kiss, but it doesn't involve as much saliva-swapping and is still really intense. Picture how your lips would be if you were drinking a bottle of water. Then take the bottle out of the equation and insert a boy. Voilà! Open-mouthed kissing. *Steaminess Factor: A+*

The Smother–Kiss: Smother-kissing is when you lean into your guy and use your whole body to kiss. It can be great, as long as you can both breathe and he doesn't reverse things and put so much weight on you that you feel like the Leaning Tower of Pisa. *Steaminess Factor: A*

The Cheek Press: This is more of a hug/kiss move than a full-on kiss. After a long makeout-style kiss, you lean in to hug your guy and press your cheek against his. It's a movie-moment and, most of the time, it's super romantic. *Steaminess Factor: B*

The Public Peck: Okay, so this isn't an advanced technique, but it's definitely essential to your kissing repertoire. It's simply a light kiss on the lips or cheek for those times when you're out in public. It's the most parent- and/or teacher-appropriate of all the types of kisses—not that you necessarily want to kiss in front of your parents or teachers. *Steaminess Factor: C*

EXTRA CREDIT

If you really want to be ready for all those kiss-worthy moments, remember a few things:

1. **Have kissable lips.** Even though 90 million American women never leave home without slicking on lipstick, 47 percent of men prefer to kiss a woman with bare lips. It's not just that guys prefer a more natural look (they think you're beautiful just the way you are); they're against lipstick and lip gloss because they make for messy kissing!

2. **Remember to breathe mid-kiss.** Unless you have a bad cold, just breathe through your nose. And you probably shouldn't kiss with a cold anyway—chances are, by the time you're feeling better, he'll be sick and passing it back to you. It's a vicious circle.

3. **Take charge.** Some guys think kissing is actually an intense game of tongue wrestling. But unless you're into slobber, you'll be better off with a good open-mouth kiss and just a touch of tongue. If he's forcing his tongue down your throat, help him out. Kiss him lightly and pull back a little. He should get the hint.

4. **Keep it special.** Even though kissing is totally fun, it's probably not a good idea to kiss every guy you hang out with. According to *Cosmopolitan* magazine, 45 percent of guys have kissed a girl whose name they couldn't remember. You don't want to be part of that statistic! You want to leave an impression. And believe me, if you really like him, your kiss will show it, and it will definitely keep him thinking about you long after he's dropped you off!

Not-So-Kiss-Worthy

Of course, not every kiss will be a memory-maker, at least not in a good way. Here are a few things to watch out for.

The Stubble Rub: Although your crush might look cute with that goatee, when it rubs against your soft lips it will feel like sandpaper on silk. Your lips can actually get a little raw from stubble rub, so if your man has a 'stache, bring along some ChapStick or tell him to go easy.

Bad Breath: Talk about a mood-killer. Bad breath is a major kissing no-no, but if he has it, you can help by supplying plenty of breath mints or breath-freshening strips. (Those things are deadly strong.) And be sure to practice the Rule of Boths: If one of you wants salsa or garlic bread at dinner, you both have salsa or garlic bread. That way, you won't notice the pungent leftover herb taste in his mouth because you'll have it, too.

The Bad-Date Chronicles

Of course, not every date ends with a perfect kiss. Bad dates happen, even to the best of us. And unless you're some sort of fortune-teller, you'll have no idea that a date is about to go bad until you're already stuck on the roller coaster, waiting for the ride to come to a complete stop. But there are a few ways to make the best of a bad date, or at least survive it. And if nothing else, sometimes a bad date makes for a really good story later.

Bad Date №1: Your Dream Date Is a Total Nightmare

You're decked out in your hottest jeans and ready for the best date of your life. Until your dream guy turns off the charm and shows his true colors. Turns out, Mr. Perfect is actually the King of Road Rage. And things don't get better once you're out of the car. He just changes his focus from the minivan that cut him off on the freeway to the waitress serving you dinner. Who does he think he is, complaining that the music is too loud, the air-conditioning too cold, and his steak too well-done? Talk about mood killer. Is there any way to salvage this date or at least enjoy the rest of your meal?

This is a good time to try out some of your most charming moves. Try to change the subject and get him talking about something that makes him happy: a movie he likes, his dog, anything. And then, when the date is over and he drops you off, run like hell! No one wants to spend time with someone who needs anger-management therapy. You have better things to do than waste another night with the most negative guy in the universe.

Bad Date №2: Boring Doesn't Even Begin to Describe It

You think you have a lot in common with this guy. Then you sit through an hour-long dinner listening to him talk about how he plans to get at least 1500 on the SAT. And then, to make matters worse, he orders dessert so he can finish giving you the tedious details of his study techniques—as if the meal hadn't been painful enough! You are about to start banging your head against the table, but don't gouge your eyes out with your dessert fork just yet. Instead, use his monotone as a backdrop for some relaxation. Breathe deep and imagine you're in a peaceful yoga studio. Flex your feet under the table and go to your happy place. Just be sure not to fall asleep!

Bad Date №3: You Feel Sick (and not in a "that-party-was-sick!" kind of way)

One holiday season, this uber-hot hockey player asked me to go with him to *The Nutcracker*. I'd been lusting after him in history class for months, and he finally wanted to take me out. I couldn't wait to get dressed up, go downtown for a swanky dinner, and have his arm around me during the ballet. Then I got the stomach flu in the middle of our date. Literally. I wasn't feeling great before he picked me up, but I figured it was predate jitters. Turns out, my rosy glow was actually a fever, and in the middle of dinner I had to excuse myself from our $30-a-plate dinner to go to the ladies' room and puke. We never made it to the ballet, and he had to pull over twice on the way home so I could throw up on the side of the road. Luckily, the hockey hottie was a total sweetheart and actually called the next day to see how I was feeling. But it wasn't a date either of us wanted to reenact. Getting sick in front of someone definitely isn't first date material.

Of course, not every date will be as understanding as mine was. If you lose your lunch mid-date and he's less than nice, consider the circumstances. Was he just a little upset because you barfed on his new silk tie, or was he pissed because you ruined his night? If his bad attitude has more to do with him being a jerk than you being queasy, then call a friend to come pick you up and consider yourself lucky that the flu saved you from a guy who doesn't have the first idea about taking care of others.

YOU WERE THERE!

Real-Life Dating Horror Stories

Three's a Crowd

"I was asked out by a guy, and we went out to dinner. He saw his ex-girlfriend there, and she decided to sit at our booth—next to me! The whole time, they talked about old memories, and when she left, she kissed him on the cheek and said she really missed what they had. Needless to say, we never went out again. I heard they got back together a week after that." —Milo, 16

Borrring!

"My worst date was actually a second date. The first date was great. The second one was so blah, I didn't even get to the third. The guy brought me to the EXACT same coffee shop, and we talked about the EXACT same things we talked about on the first date."—Courtney, 18

Too Much, Too Soon

"Basically, my worst date was when this guy told me he loved me after only three weeks of dating, and then stuck his tongue down my throat. Yuck." —Marissa, 17

Movie Drama

"My worst date was when I went to the movies with this guy. It started off nice—he paid, and we went to a movie that I wanted to see. But then, near the end of the movie, he excused himself to go to the bathroom. When he didn't come back, I started to worry that he ditched me there. I walked out of the theater and found him with another girl. He apologized, but I was mortified." —Caiti, 16

GUYS TELL IT LIKE IT IS:

Dating Around

"I haven't ever had a serious girlfriend. There's a bunch of girls I like, but I don't want to spend all my time with one person yet." —**Logan 15**

"It freaks me out when girls get clingy. I don't want them to think things are more serious than they are." —**Ross, 16**

GIRL TALK: The Process of Elimination

A lot of girls think you should look around to see what's out there before settling on one guy. That's exactly why you're studying up on how to date like an all-star!

"I think when you're a teenager you should date around to get a good idea of what you want in a guy. . . . Don't settle for Mr. Right Now; wait for Mr. Right." —**Marissa, 17**

"Going steady right now is waaay to soon!" —**Paige, 14**

"I've only ever had steady boyfriends. I dated one boy for a year and a half and another for a year and eight months. I don't think it's a good idea to get too serious too soon now that I've been there." —**Susie, 17**

Get Your Group On

Not quite ready for the intensity of a one-on-one dating situation? Fear not! Group dating is the perfect way to start the process slowly. There's none of the pressure that comes when you're alone with McDreamy, and you don't have to sit around and wait for some guy to get his act together and ask you out (or for youself to do the same). Not to mention that group dates are perfect for people whose parents won't let them "date." We'll touch on that in chapter 7.

The best thing about group dating is that it doesn't take a lot of organization on your part or your crush's. You can pull a group date together anytime you're with a bunch of people and want to go do something, because a group date is essentially that: hanging out with a group of people that just happens to include your current love interest. In fact, despite the fact that you and your crush are together in the same place (and probably flirting heavily), most guys don't consider this an official date. And that's a good thing—if he doesn't feel pressure to make things perfect, he'll be able to really focus on actually hanging out with you! Flirting tactics, here you come! The only catch is that a lot of guys are content to park themselves in front of a TV to play video games, so you might have to be the one to initiate an actual activity.

After a few group dates (a.k.a. major flirting sessions), the guy should get the hint and start planning things on his own. Hey, you've been chatting him up and spending time with him for a while now, haven't you? If he doesn't get the idea, spell it out for him. Tell your crush how fun you think it would be if everyone got together for a barbecue at the park. It will be a little encouragement to push him over the edge. If he's interested, you can even plan it together (just another way to get to know him better). Hey, you don't have a problem pitching in as long as he makes as much of an effort as you do. It's all about working together!

GIRL TALK: **Pressure-free Fun**

"Relaxing, fun dates are the best because there's no pressure. It's best to go out with a group of people in case you decide you aren't into the guy." —**Alex, 19**

Fun in Numbers: The Three Best Group Dates, for Any Season in Any City

You don't have to be in a big city to find something cool to do; you just have to think outside the box. Start off with one of these ideas, and after a few non-dinner-and-a-movie dates, you'll be coming up with your own unconventional ways to get your boy, your friends, and yourself off your butts.

1. **Go to your local zoo, planetarium, or museum.** It may sound cheesy, but there's no better place to walk around, show off your smarts, and point out things you find interesting—holding your man's hand all the while! Plus, the whole group isn't stuck in one place and, unlike at a movie, you and lover boy actually have a chance to talk to each other. Be sure to ask about student discounts because most places have cheaper ticket prices for teens.

2. **Board-game blowout.** This one does involve hanging out at someone's house, but there's nothing like a little healthy competition to spice up any night. Whether you're playing Scrabble, poker, or charades, dividing up into teams and playing to win makes for a really good time. Just don't forget the treats! Soda, chips, and M&M's are key to any game night.

3. **Live-music living.** Whether you live in Austin or Spokane, your town probably has a rockin' live-music scene, and there's nothing like a concert to get everyone having a good time. Search your weekly paper to find out where the local bands play, and then pick up some tickets to check out the next big show. You may discover that the boy next door is a great dancer and, even if he's not, you might discover the next big thing for your iPod.

e-Love

People don't just date face-to-face anymore. Between text messages, instant messaging, Facebook, and email, you spend as much time flirting with your crush online as you do in person. But what if a guy you don't know that well, a friend-of-a-friend from a rival high school, messages you on Facebook? His picture is totally hot, he likes the same movies you do, and you've heard that he's generally a nice guy. But you've never actually met him. What to do? Like anything that you do online, there are risks involved . . .

- No matter how cute his messages are, don't give away any personal details. You wouldn't give some random guy your address or phone number, so don't pass it around online. It's a good idea to keep your last name and photo private too, at least until you've spent a few months getting to know each other.

- After a few months of cyber-talking, it's probably time to talk to him on the phone. After all, messaging is great, especially if he's practically a poet, but you can learn a lot from someone's voice, and it's important that you guys can carry on a verbal conversation as well as a cyber one. Offer to call him so that you don't have to give your number out quite yet. Eventually you want to be able to talk face-to-face, right?

- Loop your parents in from the get-go. This is one of those times when the sooner they know what you're up to, the better. If you spring it on your mom that you want to go meet your "boyfriend," whom you've been seeing online for the last six months, she's going to flip. But if you've been talking about him since your first conversation, she'll be more comfortable with the idea. And be sure that if you do actually meet an online friend in person, you do it in a public place and take a parent with you. Better safe than sorry! And after you get physical proof he's a good guy, you can ditch Mom or Dad.

No matter what, be super careful about all of your online relationships. There are a lot of creeps out there. When in doubt, keep him out. Don't even start the conversation if you have any sort of bad feeling about it.

EXTRA CREDIT

Quiz: Are You a Good Date?

1. It's your first date with that hottie from world history class and he's taking you to a new sushi restaurant. You're totally decked out in your fave little black dress, and he shows up at your door wearing old army shorts. You:

   A. Panic and tell him you're suddenly not feeling well. You'll have to take a rain check.

   B. Look him up and down and ask when he decided to sign up for the National Guard.

   C. Give him a big smile and say you're ready to go. Who says he has to be in a tux every time you go out? Plus, his dimples totally make up for his ratty T-shirt.

2. Your date takes you out to a nice restaurant and tells you to order whatever you want. You know he worked two jobs over the summer to earn spending money, so you:

   A. Say you're not hungry and order a side salad to go with your ice water.

   B. Order the lobster. If he doesn't want you to order something expensive, he shouldn't offer.

   C. Order the pasta Bolognese: a mid-priced dish and just what you've been craving. Who doesn't like black olives and marinara sauce?

3. It's prom night, and you're with one of your best guy friends. He's not your true love, but you know you're going to have one of the best nights of your life. So when your crush of the last three years comes up and says you should hang out with him later, you:

A. Stammer and blush. You don't know what to say.

B. Flip your hair and ask him where he wants to meet. Your friend (a.k.a. date) can fend for himself. It's not like he was expecting anything, anyway.

C. Smile and flirt for a minute or so, but then say that you're already here with someone else. Maybe you two can meet up next weekend? You would never leave your friend hanging.

4. Your steady boyfriend picks you up in his brand-new Jetta, and even though you go out for a romantic dinner, he can't talk about anything but the car the entire night. You:

A. Just listen and nod when he asks, over appetizers, if you can feel the pickup as he accelerates. You don't know anything about cars and you don't want to sound stupid.

B. Pick a fight before the waiter even takes your order. If he thinks you're going to sit there all night while he rambles on about horsepower and torque, he's on another planet. Did he even notice that you don't have water yet?

C. Go with it—at least for tonight. Sure, his all-car talk is a little annoying, but you're happy for him and think he deserves one night to gush. It is his dream car, after all, and you do love the seat warmers. Not to mention that the chocolate sundae you ordered for dessert is divine.

5. After hanging out with a group of friends, your date tells you he has to get to bed early to be ready for the SAT tomorrow morning. Everyone else is going out for pizza, and you were counting on hanging out later than ten o'clock. You:

   A. Are disappointed but figure you can just make some mac and cheese after he drops you off.
   B. Tell him he's lame and that he's probably not going to do well on the test anyway. He can't even spell when he sends you texts!
   C. Wish him good luck on the test and tell him you can catch a ride home with someone else. You definitely want him to get a good night's sleep, and you'll save him a slice of pizza for tomorrow after he aces the test.

6. A guy from last year's Spanish class has been asking you out for months, and even though you think he's kind of a nerd, you finally say *yes.* You're out at a movie with him when your old boyfriend enters the theater with his new fling. You:

   A. Totally freeze up. Your date keeps asking what's wrong, but you can't talk about it.
   B. Make eye contact with your old man and then start nuzzling your date to make him jealous. You know he can't stand seeing you with other guys, and you look hot tonight.
   C. Wave at him and say *hi* to the girl he's with. It's not like you want to have a full-on conversation, but you might as well acknowledge the situation.

7. You're on a date at a pretty nice restaurant when your cell rings. It's your best friend; she's been on vacation; so you haven't talked to her for two weeks. You are practically hyper-ventilating—you want to talk to her so bad—but you haven't even come close to finishing your chicken. You:

A. Aren't sure what to do, and your phone rings eight times and goes to voicemail long before you make up your mind.

B. Answer the call, of course. You haven't talked to her for TWO WEEKS! Your date can't expect you to blow off your best friend.

C. Send the call to voicemail, and tell your date you're just going to send your friend a quick text to let her know what time you'll be home and can talk. You aren't about to launch into a two-hour catch-up call while at dinner with someone else.

CELL PHONE OFF

Scoring:

Mostly A's: The Scaredy-Date. You need to loosen up and stop worrying so much about being every guy's dream girl, or you're never going to have any fun. It's okay to be shy, but remember that having opinions doesn't make you impolite. Any guy who's worth your time will like a girl who can speak her mind and still respect another person's views. When you start speaking up a little, you'll be surprised to discover how much more you have to talk about.

Mostly B's: The Date-zilla. You are such a princess that it's a wonder guys are still asking you out. How can you ever expect to have a good time with someone else when everything is about you? You need to stop being so critical of the guys you go out with. And remember that, even though he asked you out, you still need to have some basic manners, or your first date with him will probably be your last.

Mostly C's: The Perfect Date! You're kind, gracious, and up for (almost) anything. Not to mention that you can have fun no matter where you are, who you're with, and what you're wearing! What guy wouldn't want to spend his spare time and hard-earned cash taking you out on the town? Just be sure you don't get so caught up in enjoying the moment that you lose track of what you want long-term. You deserve a guy who's as great a date as you!

Why is **Vanessa Minnillo** a good date? She believes in *"turning off your cell phone when you're with someone you love."* So that's the secret to nabbing a total hunk—make him think he's the only one in your world!

CELEB SHOUT-OUT!

chapter 5

THE HEART OF THE MATTER:
Love and Relationships

Eventually, if all goes well, dating leads to a relationship. But how does that happen? How do you get a relationship off the ground?

The first thing to remember when you're trying to launch a new relationship is to take it slow. This is way harder than it sounds. Whenever I was crushing on a guy, I would want to be with him 24/7, but after about three weeks, I would be bored out of my mind. Remember that you start off almost all relationships with those dizzying butterflies in your stomach. You know the symptoms: You can't stop smiling every time someone mentions his name, and you spend almost every hour of the day wishing he would call just so you could say hi. But don't ditch everything else in your life just because your few weeks of flirting have been fun.

There's no exact ratio of dating time to relationship readiness. Every couple is different, and the important thing is that you feel happy, safe, and comfortable around him. But when you are ready to take the next step, remember to ease into

the relationship. Unless you want one, it's not necessary to have an official "let's be a couple" discussion. You can let him know how you really feel in your own way. Just make sure he opens up to you, too. Take it from DJ AM: "When you like a guy, it's important to say, 'I'm falling for you,' instead of playing like you're not." Those games won't get you anywhere!

GIRL TALK: What Girls Are Looking For

"I want a guy who has an awesome sense of humor but knows how to be serious, too. We can talk to each other about anything—like best friends. When we fight, we talk it out and realize mistakes happen. He does little things, like calling just to tell me good night. We have a great time together, but we know how to be apart sometimes, too." —Liz, 17

GUYS TELL IT LIKE IT IS: Your Life Isn't a Soap Opera

"I've been with girls who are very dramatic, and to me it's a waste. When there's constant drama all the time, it's such a drain on your energy. Just enjoy each other's company. I think a lot of drama comes out of insecurity—that is probably the biggest turnoff in the entire world." —Adam Levine, singer

"Don't try to make our relationship more dramatic than it is. Why do girls want their relationships to be like soap operas? The drama is too much for me." —Joshua, 16

"Girls freak out about every little thing. Chill out. Things aren't usually that big of a deal, but they make it seem like everything is the end of the world. It really stresses me out." —Tony, 17

GRANT ON ... Why Your Guy Might Not Want a Girlfriend

In high school, I liked the idea of a girlfriend, but I didn't want it to be too serious. Not that I wanted to be a player—I just liked hanging out with my guy friends, or playing sports or video games, not really the sort of thing you share with your girlfriend. It didn't mean I didn't like a girl if I didn't want her to be my "girlfriend," it just meant I wasn't ready for anything super serious.

Four Tips for a Rewarding Relationship

A good relationship is all about balance. Picture a teeter-totter with you at one end and your man at the other. The goal is to keep you both up in the air without one flying off while the other hits the ground with a thump. These four tips are like seat cushions on your teeter-totter—they're essential for good balance and a comfortable ride!

1. *Agree to disagree.* It might sound like something from *7th Heaven*, but this is actually really good advice. No matter how in love you are, you are still two different people, which means you're bound to sometimes have two different opinions. Don't let the fact that you think omelets are a breakfast-only food and he thinks they're perfectly suited to dinner get in the way of an otherwise good thing. Let those small disagreements go, and if you can't, find someone who feels the same way about omelets as you do.

2. Love him for who he is. No matter how much it might drive you crazy that he wears his favorite hideous baseball cap every single day, don't say anything mean about it. If you really can't stand it, get him a hat that you'll both like for his birthday. Otherwise, get over it. It's just a hat; you're dating the guy underneath it. The same goes for all the other little things that annoy you—they're part of who he is, and you don't want to change that. Not only are those little things the reason you fell for him in the first place, but the last thing you want is for him to become a clone. (He shouldn't try to change you either. Who cares if he likes it when you wear heels? If you're a flats girl then you should keep on rocking those shoes, and he should be happy about it.)

3. Bring out his inner feminist. Any guy who thinks *feminism* is a bad word is still living in the dark ages. Why would your boyfriend want you to be anything less than the smart, independent, driven woman you are? He should be proud that his lady has a mind of her own. Make sure any guy you date really respects you. You deserve nothing less.

4. Just be yourself! I know, I know. So motherly. But seriously, why would you ever want to be with a guy who doesn't know who you really are? Acting like someone else is totally exhausting, and you are plenty cool just being you. If a guy can't recognize that, he's not worth the time it takes to dial his number. At the end of the day, if you don't have anything in common with a guy, you probably won't have fun in the relationship. He's not going to seem very cute when you're so bored that you can't remember how to spell your own last name. Save yourself (and him) the trouble and just be up front about who you really are from the start.

Will Act for Love

One of my good friends, Amanda, got stuck in an acting-for-love situation. Our entire senior year, she was truly, madly, deeply in love with Nick. He was good-looking, kind of geek-cool, and totally into video games, '70s punk rock, and comic books. Amanda, on the other hand, was into ballet, retro '80s tunes, and Jane Austen. But because she liked Nick so much, she got into video games, punk music, and graphic novels, and seemed to forget about the things that used to interest her. (I almost passed out when I showed up at her house one day and they were watching that Japanese cartoon *Akira*.) And it worked—for a while.

Fast-forward six months. Nick and Amanda had officially been a couple for almost four months, but it turned out that no matter how hard she tried, she couldn't force herself to like mountain biking or playing random shoot-the-bad-guy computer games. Nick honestly couldn't figure out what her deal was, and after a few weeks of fighting, they broke up. But that wasn't the worst part. Nick's next girlfriend, Sophie, was someone we often saw at the same movies and hanging out at the same places as we did. She genuinely liked a lot of the same things Amanda did, like folk music and basketball. The difference was that Sophie wasn't afraid to be herself, and Nick liked her for that. Amanda didn't even give Nick the chance to get to know the real her; if she had, she and Nick might have had something really great. He hadn't liked the real Amanda because he hadn't ever met her.

Lesson learned. Amanda's next boyfriend, a hottie who lived down the hall during her sophomore year of college, got to know the real her: They're still together.

Take it from Avril Lavigne (and Amanda): "If there is a guy you like, and you feel like you have to dress a certain way to get him to like you, the relationship won't work out. Because you need to be able to be yourself around him."

"If you try to be someone you think a guy wants, he won't get to know the real you. I used to think I wasn't good enough, so I'd tell a white lie to seem 'better.' Then I realized that by not being myself, I was taking away her choice to decide whether she actually liked me." —DJ AM

"I love a girl with a good sense of humor who doesn't take herself too seriously." —Enrique Iglesias, singer

"I feel like everyone has something cool to offer. But I do like girls who are funny. You don't have to be hilarious, but at least enjoy humor. Nothing's more annoying to me than hanging out with someone who doesn't get when you're joking. It's the biggest buzz kill." —Adam Brody, actor

Romance Doesn't Require Limos, Roses, or Candlelit Tables for Two

Just because you don't have the budget for a *Sex and the City*–style night on the town doesn't mean you can't feel the love. Start your romantic rendezvous off with one of these ideas.

Make-your-own-meal magic. You don't need reservations at the hottest new restaurant to have a romantic dinner. In fact, making your man a special meal is one of the most thoughtful ways to show him you care. Fix his favorite food and then sit down together to enjoy it. If you're not sure of his favorite or don't know how to prepare foie gras, just cook something you both like—a good steak and hot fudge sundae will make almost any guy drool!

Watch a romantic movie. There's nothing like a little on-screen love to set the mood! Set your Netflix to send you a classic movie like *Ghost* or *Dirty Dancing*, curl up with a blanket and some popcorn, and voilà—instant romance!

Go for a hike under the stars. Leave it to Mother Nature to set the stage for a romantic night. Whether you set out a blanket at a local park or actually head out into the wild to get away from the city lights, a starlit night can inspire almost any couple.

Take a walk down memory lane. If you've been dating someone for a while and have had one or two dates that really stick out, take your man for a "best of" trip through your relationship. Reenact your fave date, whether it was hanging out watching a football game on TV or getting gelato at an authentic Italian restaurant, and watch him melt.

The L-Word

No, not *lesbian*. We're talking about *love*. It's a four-letter word that can get more of a reaction than any of the others. Saying it to a boyfriend is a big step. Just like you want to take your time getting into a relationship, you want to take some time in the relationship before dropping the *L*-bomb. Saying it too early can put a lot of pressure on both of you, sometimes even ruining the relationship. Wait until you have been together long enough, usually four to six months. Then, not only will it really mean something, but you'll know each other well enough to express your true feelings.

GRANT ON ... Love

I never told a girl I loved her in high school. And, looking back, I think I made the right call. There's plenty of time to get serious without rushing things. If some guy starts telling you he loves you after a few dates, he's probably trying to get something out of you. Most guys don't fall in love after just a few dates.

How Do I Love Thee?

You are totally crazy about him and you know you're in love. What else could make you want to tell the whole planet how amazing he is? He's practically all you can think about, and you're ready to tell him how you feel. But how is he going to react? Here are a few possible responses and how you can handle them.

A. He totally clams up. He's probably intimidated by the idea of love. You know how, in movies, guys act like being in love means you have to get married, get a dog, and start working as an accountant? That's not what you're saying at all. If you say something specific, like "I love you because you make me laugh," or "I love how you always sing along to the radio," your guy will be able to see that love in real life isn't like the movies, and it can work in whatever kind of relationship you two have.

B. He says, "I love you, too." Bingo! He's willing to talk about how he feels and obviously is smart enough to be as crazy about you as you are about him. Enjoy the moment!

C. He smiles and/or blushes. He's probably nervous because saying "I love you" is a big step, and he's not ready to go there yet. But the fact that he's nervous shows he doesn't want to hurt your feelings and obviously really cares about you. Don't pressure him to say something he doesn't mean. Chances are, if you ask whether he feels the same way, he'll say yes—even if it's not true. (How many guys do you know who would say no in a moment like that?) Instead, ease the moment by giving him a little kiss and sharing a good memory, like the time you guys went to shoot hoops and ended up spending the whole afternoon hanging out in the park. He'll say it when he's ready.

EXTRA CREDIT *Want to Spice Up the Way You Say "I Love You"?*

Try whispering those magic words in your boyfriend's ear in a different language! Here are 20 options to get you started.

- **Arabic:** Ana ahebak (*on-uh ah-bok*)
- **Chinese (Mandarin):** Wo ai ni (*woe eye nee*)
- **Dutch:** Ik hou van jou (*eek how van yo*)
- **Finnish:** Minä rakastan sinua (*meen-ah rock-aus-tin seen-ohh-ahh*)
- **French:** Je t'aime (*zhuh tem*)
- **German:** Ich liebe Dich (*eesh lee-bah deesh*)
- **Greek:** S'agapo (*suh-gop-oh*)
- **Hawaiian:** Aloha wau ia`oe (*uh-low-ha wow ay oi*)
- **Hindi:** Mai tumse pyar karta hoo (*May tomb-say puh-yar cur-tuh who*)
- **Hungarian:** Szeretlek (*Sar-et-leck*)
- **Indonesian:** Aku sayang padamu (*ack-oo su-young pa-duh-moo*)
- **Italian:** Ti amo (*tee ahh-moe*)
- **Japanese:** Aishitemasu (*eye-sh-tay-ma-su*)
- **Korean:** Sarang hae (*saw-ron yay*)
- **Polish:** Kocham cie (*co-ham che*)

Romanian: Te iubesc (*teh you-besk*)

Russian: Ya tyebya lyublyu (*Yah tey-bee-ah lay-blue*)

Sign language: Spread your hand out so that no fingers are touching. With your palm facing away from your body, bring in your middle and ring fingers and touch them to the palm of your hand.

Spanish: Te amo (*tay ahh-moe*)

Swahili: Naku penda (*Knock-eww pen-dah*)

I LOVE YOU

When Your Boyfriend Is Older:

THE DOS AND DON'TS OF DATING OLDER GUYS

My friend Elizabeth has this theory about guys who go out with girls who are years younger than they are. Here's what she thinks:

"Guys who go for younger girls are the losers who can't get girls their own age. Every time I see some twenty-year-old schmuck with a cute sixteen-year-old girl, I want to stop them on the street and say to her, 'Do you know who he is? He's that guy in your grade. (And here I'd point to a guy who's the same age as the girl but whom she would never date.) 'Would you ever date him? I didn't think so.' I think if girls could see older guys in the context of their own age groups, they would have a totally different impression of them."

Elizabeth is on to something. A lot of older guys like dating younger girls because it makes them feel powerful and manly, whatever that means. And I can sort of see the attraction for girls. It's nice to be with someone who has some extra cash, owns a car, and seems to know how the world works. But you don't want to be with someone solely because he was born a few years before you were, so before you start dating an older guy, make sure he passes this three-question test.

1. Do my friends and family like him?

Your BFF and parents would never want you to get hurt, so listen to and trust them when they start warning you about a guy.

2. Does he pressure me to do anything I don't want to do and make me feel young or scared if I don't give in?

That's a power play, and it's a big scary warning sign. Just because you're younger than a guy doesn't give him the right to make you second-guess yourself or feel like a baby—ever! Get out of that situation ASAP.

3. Would I still date him if he were in my grade?

I call this one the Elizabeth test. Look to see which guys your age he most resembles and, if you'd date one of them, chances are he is your type.

Dating Around: You're Not a Player, You Just Crush a Lot

Relationships aren't for everyone (see Grant's thoughts on page 83), and there's no reason you should feel any pressure to stick with one guy if that's not what you want to do. And even if you are a relationship kind of girl, how are you supposed to find the guy of your dreams without considering a few possibilities? But, for some reason, girls who date around often get stuck with a bad rep.

You know how it goes. A guy goes out with four girls in one weekend and he's "the man." But if a girl does that, she's considered a slut. Hello?! What happened to equality of the sexes?

The key to keeping things on an even footing is to make sure you don't have double standards: Don't let guys get away with things that you wouldn't let girls get away with, good or bad. And be sure to remember that dating around is a lot different from sleeping around. If people tell you otherwise, they're probably insecure about their own dating situation. Besides, no one but you really knows what's going on with any of your dates. Maybe you just like flirting and hanging out. Or maybe you're just trying a few guys on for size! As long as you're comfortable with your behavior, and you're sure that it doesn't compromise who you are, why should you care what other people think? Tell anyone who gives you a hard time to deal with it or move on. Or better yet, ignore them and enjoy yourself.

Something else to keep in mind: Oftentimes, guys take their cues from girls, so if you call other girls names, chances are the guys will, too. You have to be the good example. Don't let guys you know get away with name-calling or girl-bashing of any kind. If you hear a boy say something nasty about another girl, call him on it. He should know better.

CELEB SHOUT-OUT!

"Date lots of people and have lots of experiences. That's the beauty of being single: The world is really your oyster." —Sarah Jessica Parker, actress

Off the Hook:
Hooking Up ≠ Relationship

Hooking up is one of those gray areas in dating and relationships. Actually, it's one of the grayest. People "hook up" all the time, but do you really even know what hooking up means? Is there a set definition in the dictionary or on Wikipedia? Not one that really explains what you need to know. But some cool girls from four different states offer insight:

"Hooking up is making out but it's really casual. If you're hooking up with a guy, he's not your boyfriend." —Lila, 16, Michigan

"Hooking up is the same as 'friends with benefits.'"
—Pam, 18, New Jersey

"Your hook-up buddy is someone you make out with when you don't have a boyfriend. He's a friend, but you guys aren't committed or anything. It's not like he's going to ask you to prom." —Kitty, 16, Texas

"No one I know really hooks up with strangers. It's usually someone they know from school, and they just kind of make out for a night."
—Nicole, 15, Utah

Guys view hooking up in pretty much the same way:

"Hooking up is what you do when you think a girl is hot, but you don't want to have to take her to dinner. Sometimes it's making out. Sometimes it's a little more." —Ethan, 17, Texas

"I've hooked up with three girls, but a lot of my friends have hooked up with way more girls than that. Hooking up means you get some action, but you don't have to deal with girl drama." —Liam, 17, California

"I once hooked up with my best friend, but I wish I hadn't. It totally changed everything, and she started hating me." —Jake, 16, Connecticut

Okay, that helps a little, but it's still kind of fuzzy, right? That's because everyone has a different definition. There is one thing however all the girls and guys I interviewed agreed on: Hooking up is meant to be casual. You hook up when you want to have a good time but don't want to commit. You are not exclusive, so you can "hook up" with one guy on a Friday night, and the next night, hook up with someone completely new. There's no guarentee he'll be your boyfriend or even hook up with you again. There's no commitment at all.

At the end of the day, hooking up isn't a new phenomenon. People have been making out without commitment for years. But lately, hooking up among teens is getting a lot of attention. Why is everyone (parents in particular) getting so worked up?

As fun as it is, letting someone kiss and touch you is a big deal, and if it were up to your parents you'd only make out with people you care about and who care about you. An old-fashioned idea, maybe, but your parents don't want you to get hurt—physically or emotionally. Plus, they think you're too special to hook up with any random guy, and they're hoping you think so, too. You can essentially break your parent's concerns down into four words: Don't sell yourself short.

It's important to remember that, by definition, hook-ups don't lead to boyfriends. So if you like a guy and want to go out with him, make an effort to really get to know him. Rushing into things can make those getting-to-know-you stages awkward, and it's hard to know if a guy really respects you or is just interested in more hook-ups if you haven't taken the time to hang out first. Don't be afraid to tell an eager guy to slow it on down. If he's really interested in you, he'll take things at your pace. And if he won't slow down, keep looking for someone who will.

At the end of the day, *you* have to decide what you want your relationships to be. You have to set the terms—with boyfriends, hook-up partners, or anyone else—because otherwise someone else will set them for you.

EXTRA CREDIT

Hooking up means different things to different people, but what's really important is what it means to you. Figure out your own definition, whether it's based on past experience, what your friends think, your own imagination, or a combination of all these things. It's good to keep your own definition in your back pocket for the next time some guy asks if you'd like to hook up—that way you know what it really means to you before you even go there.

chapter 6

YOU WEAR THE PANTS:
Setting Your Boundaries

When it comes to your body and how your guy treats you, you call the shots. No ifs, ands, or buts. After all, it's your body, and you are in charge of it. That's why you need sexual and physical boundaries—so it's clear to anyone you date what you do and don't want.

The word *boundary* can sound like a restriction, as if by setting boundaries you would be limiting yourself. Actually, knowing what you are comfortable with is really liberating—you don't have the stress of making a decision in the heat of the moment, when lines are blurred and your defenses might be down. And you don't have to worry about waking up feeling guilty or cheap (which you aren't), because you know how far you are willing to go before you cross any lines.

Create your own boundaries based on what you believe, what you'll accept, and what you won't tolerate. Your boundaries are a large part of who you are, which is why it's so important that guys respect them.

That's all fine and good in theory; we've all gotten the birds-and-the-bees talk from our parents or in health class. But how can you actually be clear about your boundaries with your latest crush without seeming like a prude or scaring him off? Don't all guys want just one thing (a.k.a. sex)?

In a good relationship, your boyfriend *will* want just one thing: for you to be happy. And you aren't going to be happy going further than you're ready to go, no matter how in love you are or how much he wants you.

My dad always used to tell me that guys were after just one thing. (Here we go with the one thing again.) And even though not every guy I dated was in it for the action, there were a few who liked me, but not enough to listen when I said no. And frankly, that's not acceptable. Those aren't the kinds of guys you want to be with. A real relationship, whether you're 16 or 40, is based on respect and trust. How can you trust a guy who doesn't respect you enough to stop pressuring you to go further than you're ready to? How can you ever really be yourself if you aren't sure what he's really after?

A guy who's really worth your time will want a relationship with you before he even knows what the "benefits" will be. A guy who is worthy of you will think *you* are the real benefit.

GUYS TELL IT LIKE IT IS:

Staying within the Limits

"I would never push a girl further than she wanted to go."
—Jameson, 16

"It's actually easier when a girl says what her boundaries are when you first start going out. That way you know, and you don't have to guess what she wants." —Campbell, 17

GRANT ON ...Respect

I was always very respectful of the lines girls had set up. All my friends were the same way. Sure, I had moments when I could barely keep my hands off my girlfriend—every guy does—but I didn't want to do anything to break her heart. And going further than she was ready to would've totally changed our relationship. I kept that in mind when we were going at it.

Guys with character, the guys you want to date, will have no problem with your boundaries. In a good relationship, you won't be the only one drawing the line—your boyfriend should help you rather than constantly trying to trip you up or move things too fast in the heat of the moment. If he's not helping, take a long look at him and think about whether he really wants what's best for you.

Walk the Line

Long before you get into a situation where you have to make that call, decide for yourself what your physical and emotional boundaries are. Draw some distinct lines in your mind so that when you and your crush are making out but you aren't ready to go any further, you know where making out ends and the next step begins. It's almost like mapping out your personal war zones: When you're in enemy territory, where is your safe ground? What are the best ways to retreat when you're in a dangerous area? You would never leave town for a road trip without a map or full tank of gas, so why enter a relationship without knowing where you want it to go? Trust yourself and your gut feelings. Do you like spending time with him but want to take things slowly? Do you feel like you want to get to know him better or go on a certain number of dates before you kiss him? Really think it through. Write about it in your journal if that will help. But remember, it's all about what feels right for you.

Hey, You!

After you've come to your own decisions about your personal boundaries, you'll need to lay them out, loud and clear, for your boyfriend. It's not fair to expect him to stay within your limits if you haven't said what they are. You might want to sit down and have an official talk, or you might feel more comfortable mentioning how you feel while you're driving to the movies. Just be sure to tell him flat out, for instance, that you think making out with him is amazing, but that's all you're comfortable with. He might be disappointed, but he'll get over it. Just be firm and don't let that cute grin convince you to do anything you don't want to do. If he's really a guy you want to be with, he'll respect you enough to stay within your boundaries and won't push you past them—ever.

If you are already in a relationship and aren't sure what you want or haven't really thought about your boundaries, ask your boyfriend to give you some time. Tell him you need to figure things out before you take the next step. Don't feel rushed just because you didn't plan for this. It's never too late to take a deep breath and figure out what's best for you.

Two-Way Street

It goes against the stereotype, but girls aren't the only ones who have boundaries. Remember that it's important to respect your boyfriend's boundaries if you expect him to respect yours. When you sit down to talk about your limits, be sure to ask him if there are things he's uncomfortable with. Being open about how you both feel will bring you closer together and make your relationship stronger.

No Means No

It's something you've probably heard before: *No* means *no*. There's not much else to say about it. It's not something that takes a lot of explanation; you don't need a master's degree to figure it out. Your body belongs to you, and if you decide you don't want someone touching it or even standing too close to it, that's your right.

When you tell a guy no about anything, he needs to listen. *No* doesn't mean "Maybe if you keep going, I'll give in," or "I'm just teasing." *No* means "If you don't stop this very second, I'm going to kick your ass." So don't be afraid to say it, don't worry about being polite or hurting his feelings, and don't be afraid to defend yourself if you don't get an immediate response. *No* doesn't need any translation, so it shouldn't take a guy more than a second to figure out what you mean. If he doesn't stop right away, yell, scream, embarrass him if you're in public, hit him, do whatever you have to do. You said *no*, and he didn't listen.

Ways to Say No

In addition to the obvious and very effective "No," there are additional things you can say to make it clear you mean business. Here are a few:

"Get your hands off me!"

"Don't touch me!"

"Stop it."

"I'm not enjoying this."

"I don't want to do this."

"If you don't stop right now, I'm leaving."

But remember, nothing hits home as well as "No!" screamed at the top of your lungs.

Pulling Out the No

Abby had been with her boyfriend for about three months when she pulled out her No. Jeff was one of those guys that lots of girls wanted: He was a captain of the football team and got good grades in all honors classes. Not to mention, he was six feet tall and gorgeous. Abby was crazy about him.

Of course, sports weren't the only thing Jeff was good at. He was an amazing kisser, and making out with him made Abby feel almost dizzy. But she had decided before they got serious that she wasn't ready for anything more than a good make-out sesh. Then, one night, things really got going. The first few times Jeff started to feel up her shirt, Abby just pushed his hands away. Then he got a little more aggressive and really started kissing her. Obviously, moving his hands away wasn't a clear enough signal, so Abby pulled her mouth away from his and said, "No. If you don't stop, I'm leaving."

That was crystal clear. Jeff immediately started apologizing and Abby made it clear, again, what her boundaries were.

They ended up dating for another four months, and Jeff never pushed her like that again—Abby wouldn't have put up with it if he had. In fact, one night Jeff was the one who pulled away. He told Abby that if they didn't stop for a second, he wasn't sure he would be able to stop himself. Jeff was one of the good guys. Every girl deserves a guy who will respect her like that.

CELEB SHOUT-OUT!

"*Know your worth. The day you settle for less is the day you will get less.*" —*Iman, supermodel*

"*When it comes to guys . . . refuse to compromise your principles.*" —*Fergie, singer*

Actor **Zac Efron** once said that the best advice his mom ever gave him was to *"treat women with respect."* All guys (and moms) should be like that!

Self-Protection

Unfortunately, not every guy is like Jeff. Although the majority of guys you'll meet will respect your boundaries and your body, there are a few who won't keep their hands to themselves. You need to be very wary of these guys and protect yourself. Here are a few things to remember in any situation, whether it's a group get-together, a one-on-one date, or just general hanging out.

1. *Trust yourself and your instincts.* If you feel weird about something, then something is probably weird. Go with that!

2. *Don't go out alone with someone you don't know* or someone who makes you feel uneasy. Use your friends or a group activity as an excuse to be with other people. It might sound outdated, but there is safety in numbers.

3. *Don't hang out at his place,* or yours, if your parents or siblings aren't around—again, the safety in numbers thing.

4. *Don't hesitate to speak up.* If someone invades your personal space, firmly tell him that he is too close and that he should step back. A loud "you're a little close for comfort" is a good way of saying *back off.* If he keeps going, make a scene to get some help.

5. *Be aware of what's going on around you.* Drugs and drinking can impair your awareness of your surroundings and your ability to protect yourself.

6. **Program the number** for your local taxi service into your phone, and always have money for a taxi. It's important that, if you get uncomfortable, you have a way out of the situation, even if you don't have a car.

7. **Take a self-defense course.** You'll learn some skills and techniques that will be good to have in your back pocket, and the class also might be a good way to get some exercise.

When No Doesn't Work

If someone doesn't respect it when you say no, he is a predator. *Predator* might sound like a harsh word, but according to a recent National Crime Victimization Survey, nearly two-thirds of reported rapes are committed by someone the victim knows personally. Just because you know the guy who forces you to have sex or perform a sexual act doesn't mean he's not a predator.

Rape is very real, and teenagers are particularly at risk. An informational service provided by the Rape Treatment Center at Santa Monica–UCLA Medical Center, 911rape reports some scary stats when it comes to teens and rape: *Most teenagers who are raped or sexually assaulted are victimized by someone they know.*

These stats aren't meant to freak you out so much that you never leave the house, but they do show how important it is for you to be hyperaware of your surroundings, no matter who you're with or what you're doing. Do everything you can to keep yourself from getting into a precarious situation.

At the same time, know that you can't always stop a predator. You can be sexually assaulted or raped even though you've done everything you know to protect yourself. It's important to remember that if you are a victim, it is NOT your fault. You have nothing to be ashamed of and have done nothing wrong. Rape is a felony, regardless of whether you know the rapist or not. Remember that you are the victim of a crime. You aren't alone, and there are ways to get help.

If you or someone you know has been raped . . .

If you are hurt or the rape has just happened, call 9-1-1 or the police. The hospital's professionals can help take care of you and will likely run tests, not only to try to catch the rapist but also to make sure you're going to be okay.

Tell someone you trust. A friend, family member, the police, or a rape crisis counselor can help you with all the physical and emotional effects of rape. Being assaulted is not something you can just "get over."

Call a rape crisis hotline or seek professional help. Nearly all cities and states have rape crisis centers, and you can find one on the Internet by searching "rape crisis" and your location. You can also find local rape crisis hotlines in your telephone directory or by calling 4-1-1.

There are also national networks that allow you to get information and help anonymously:

The Rape, Abuse, and Incest National Network (RAINN) is a national victim assistance organization with a free, confidential, 24-hour National Sexual Assault hotline. You can call 1-800-656-HOPE or go to the Web site at www.rainn.org. RAINN can help connect you to a rape crisis center in your area.

911rape is another more anonymous way to learn how to get help after an assault. Visit their Web site at: www.911rape.org.

EXTRA CREDIT

Right now, save your local taxi service's phone number in your cell phone. Then text it to all of your friends so they'll have it, too.

chapter 7

OUTSIDE FORCES:
Friends, Parents, and Other Factors

Imagine that you and your boyfriend are riding a bus. You're riding along, hanging out in the back with plenty of room to stretch out and do your own thing, until WHAM! the bus stops downtown and picks up ten people. And then ten more people. And ten more. Within a few stops, you and your boyfriend are crammed against the door like sardines. Talk about stifling!

Sometimes your relationships can feel a little like that jam-packed bus: Your parents and friends can be like the passengers getting on and pushing you up against the door. They can definitely be a good part of the ride, as long as there are seats on your bus for all of them. But without space and balance, you'll feel like you're always pushed up against the door.

Girl Power

Girlfriends are absolutely, positively essential when it comes to guys. Why? Because they're the ones who are going to be there if he dumps you—or you dump him. Good friends will stick by you through thick and thin—and many, many boyfriends. They're your support system, and no single relationship is worth ditching everyone you love. Plus, a good boyfriend would never ask you to do that. Your guy should want you to have girlfriends, and if he's mature enough, he won't feel threatened when you spend time with them. Hey, he should have friends, too! You would never ask him to ditch his posse.

Girl Fight

If you've seen *Mean Girls* or spent one day in any high school, you know how rough girl world can be, and guys seem to be the reason for a lot of the competition. But no man, unless he's some sort of well-rounded God (and chances are, he's not), is worth fighting over. There are more than three BILLION guys in the world, plenty to go around.

The first rule of girl-dom is this: Never, ever go after your friend's boyfriend.

The second rule of girl-dom is this: Never, ever go after your friend's boyfriend. Ever.

Pretty simple, right? Unfortunately, some girls don't live by the rules of girl world, and there might come a day when one of these girls starts hitting on your man. But before you start an all-out catfight, take a deep breath and a step back.

112

If she really is hitting on your boyfriend, she's one of three things:

1. *Really into him and trying to get to you*
2. *Really into him and oblivious*
3. *Not into him and trying to get to you*

If you get right down to it, number one and number three are really the same thing. This girl wants to get under your skin, and she sees your boyfriend as a way to do that. But what's really going on here? Chances are, she's insecure and threatened by you for some reason. Maybe it's your looks or your grades or your friends, or a combination of all these and more. Whatever the reason, competition and insecurity are probably fueling her flirt-attack on your boyfriend.

Here's where you have to ask yourself if you're as insecure as she is, or if you're comfortable enough with yourself and with your relationship to ignore her flirting and move on. If you know your boyfriend likes you (and why shouldn't he?), and you like him, then don't worry about some random mean girl stepping in on that.

CELEB SHOUT-OUT!

"Friendship is rarer than love." —Charles Péguy, French poet

GIRL TALK:

Don't Play in Your Friend's Backyard

"If one of my friends likes a guy first, the rest of us leave him alone." —**Marta, 15**

"My friends and I have a rule. Ex-boyfriends and crushes are dubbed and branded to that girl." —**Madeline, 18**

"There aren't any guys worth fighting over—now or ever." —**Lacey, 17**

"Sometimes you'll get catty and fight with your friends over boys, but you'll later regret it. You'll realize that arguing about a guy just gives him the power to decide which girl he wants to be with instead of you deciding if he's really worth fighting for. . . . The silly competition isn't necessary." —Fergie, singer

Two-Timing: When You and Your Friend Want the Same Guy

When a good friend is crushing on the same guy as you, you have a whole different situation on your hands. Since you don't want to ruin a friendship over some boy, you need to level with each other. Why do you like him so much? Is he really worth fighting over?

Your best bet is to both call it quits. Trying to decide who should get a shot at one guy is like trying to split an ice cream cone—it always gets messy. Instead, go out together and try to meet some new guys, or find other people at school to hang out with. Doing it together will be more fun, and chances are you'll end up discovering a few guys who are way better than the guy who started the whole thing anyway.

ADVICE FROM SOMEONE WHO'S BEEN THERE

"I have great friends, and we all operate under the rule that if someone has feelings for a guy, the others back off. If there's a situation where two friends are attracted to someone at the same time, there's open communication about it. I just think if you have to fight for a guy with your friend, she probably isn't really your friend. You should be able to talk about things before it gets to the point where you fight about it." —Aurora, 23

When Your Friends Hate Your Man

There's nothing worse than having your best friend bash the boy you've spent the last six weeks crushing on. Friends are supposed to be happy for you when things work out with a guy, aren't they? Why can't they just give you, and him, a break? Usually, when your friends start dissing your boyfriend, it's for one of three reasons.

1. They think he's bad for you. You'll know if this is the reason because your friends probably won't be quiet about it. If they've ever said anything like "You can do so much better," or "I just don't think he's right for you," or "Girl, he is bad news," they are obviously worried about you dating him.

Before you start flipping out about having your own life and making your own decisions, take a second to think about why they're so concerned. They are your friends after all, and they want the best for you.

Does your boyfriend treat you badly? Have you started doing things you would never have done before you started dating him? It's never worth it to change yourself for a guy, and no guy should EVER abuse you (emotionally, mentally, or physically), so if any of these things are going on, you should take your friends' advice and ditch him. If not, you'll need to have a heart-to-heart to find out why they are against him. If their feelings are unfounded, a good girl-talk session should be able to work out the issues and get things back on solid ground.

2. They are jealous of the time you give him. It's normal for your girl-friends to feel a little threatened when a new guy starts taking up all your time. They enjoy your company (and they should!), and you're one of the main players in your group of friends. If they start acting jealous, it's probably because they miss you and just want you around more.

The easiest way to fix the jealousy scenario is to spend more time with your gal pals. Not only will they be happier about your relationship, but your relationship will be happier. Spending some time away from Prince Charming will give your love life some balance and will make you appreciate each other more. And just imagine how happy he's going to be to see you if you don't spend every waking minute with him!

3. One of them has a thing for him. If it's one friend in particular that spends her time saying you should break up with the boyfriend in question, consider (in your mind, not out loud) if she might have a thing for him. This is very rarely the case, since most girls are loyal to their friends over any guy, but it is a possibility. If after a lot of thought, you think she's crushing on your man, you need to talk to her. But DO NOT bring it up by saying something like, "Get your hands off my guy." This will only ruin your friendship. She probably doesn't even realize that she likes him, or she's trying to hide it, so you need to give her a chance to get over it and be a decent friend. If, after you tell her all the reasons he's good for you, she continues to diss him, you'll have to decide whether to tune her out or count her out. Since friendships usually last longer than relationships, give it as long as you can before ruining your friendship over a guy. But if she's way out of line and can't be nice to you, then maybe she's not such a good friend anyway.

HE'S NO GOOD FOR YOU.

GIRLFRIENDS
GET TO KNOW YOUR GUY

1. *Start small.* Instead of bringing your boyfriend along when you're with six of your best friends (talk about overwhelming!), invite him to come over and watch a movie with two friends. A smaller group will be less intimidating and will give everyone a better chance to actually get to know one another.

2. *When you're all together,* bring up topics you know will interest both your boyfriend and your friends. Is there a movie you've all seen? Are you all *Guitar Hero* pros? Find something that works for everyone and go with that.

3. *Plan a no-pressure activity,* like bowling. Everyone will be able to talk to one another, and the bowling will help break up any awkward pauses. Plus, how many people are actually good at bowling? Chances are slim that anyone will be a pro, so it's a good way to take competition out of the situation.

4. *Have some of your friends and some of his friends* over to watch a basketball game on TV. Having people there who already like your boyfriend (in addition to you) will help defuse the situation, and your girlfriends will probably be on their best behavior if there are new guys around.

Important Friendship Factor: Do unto Others . . .

You know how much it kills you when a friend bashes your boyfriend. Remember that feeling when considering telling your friend you don't care for her new guy; unless you think he's dangerous, keep it to yourself.

When Your Boyfriend Disses Your Gal Pals

Whether he's just teasing or actually hates them, it's never cool for your man to make fun of your friends. They're your girls! How would he feel if you started ripping on his pals?

If he crosses the line and says something rude about one of your friends, it's up to you to set the record straight and defend them. You don't have to flip out right away—start by saying something like "So not cool. I don't make fun of your friends! " By showing him what he's doing without getting defensive, you're saying that you won't stand for mistreatment of your friends and that you'll show him the same respect.

The Parent Trap: Mom, Dad, and Lover Boy

Your friends aren't the only people you'll have to deal with when it comes to your man. If you saw the Ben Stiller movie *Meet the Parents*, you know how terrifying it can be for a guy to meet Mom and Dad. (Admit it: It's terrifying for you, too.) But if you really care about this guy, you'll probably want to introduce him to your parents at some point. And that's a good thing. Then your mom can see how cute he is, and your dad will see that he doesn't have a full-body tattoo. (If he does have full-sleeve tattoos and your parents are conservative types, suggest he wear a sweater—at least for the first meet-and-greet session. No need to aggravate an already tense situation.)

GRANT ON . . . Meeting the Parents

Meeting a girl's parents is by far the worst part of any date. Dads are usually worse than moms. Dads kind of stare you down, and you're already nervous, so you stammer and look like an idiot. Actually, I think dads kind of like that. I wish I could've taken the "meeting the parents" step out of every single date I ever went on, but it's a necessary evil. And once I won over a girl's mom, I was pretty much in the clear.

How to Keep Him from Getting Grilled at the Door

Before you have a guy over for an official family get together, he'll probably swing by the house to pick you up a few times. And if your parents are at all overprotective (a.k.a. normal), they'll be waiting by the door.

You might be tempted to have him call you when he's a block away so you can run out the door and jump in the car, but this is actually a bad move—worse for him than for you. Your parents will wonder why you feel you have to hide him. And it will look like he's trying to hide something. (Can't you see your parents devising a list of evidence that he's up to no good?) Instead, give your parents some ground rules for meeting McDreamy at the door.

1. Twenty Questions is out of the question. You can't veto all questions, because it's in your parents' natures to be curious, and they'll want to know something about this guy before he takes you away for the evening. Telling them they aren't allowed to ask him anything is basically giving them permission to pull out the lie-detector test and give him the full CIA interrogation. Instead, take charge and lead the question-asking session.

When your man comes to the door, say you want him to meet your parents really quickly. (It's okay to give him one of those looks that says "I have to do this," as long as your parents don't see it.) Then make the introductions by saying things like "Mom, this is Ben. We have biology together, and he's on the volleyball team." Your mom will practically be forced to ask him about volleyball because it's only polite. Try the same thing with your dad. "Dad, Ben and I are going to see the new Brad Pitt movie. Didn't you love his last one?" And voilà! Your dad will start talking about Mr. Pitt. Then it's time to get out of there before more questions ensue!

2. Gushing is for girls. Milly, 17, says her biggest fear bringing guys home is "making sure my mom doesn't gush on about how cute he is . . . right in front of him!" Sure, he's a total hottie. But how embarrassing if your parents want to take pictures or say what a cute couple you make. You're just going on a date! Lay the ground rule that no cameras or over-the-top compliments are allowed within 10 feet of the date-introduction zone until at least your fifth date or the prom. By then, the guy will know your parents are a little crazy and will probably think they're funny. If not, he's probably not the one for you anyway. After all, you can break up with him, but not with your with parents.

3. Stand-up comedy is *NOT* funny. You know how guys will sometimes make jokes because they're nervous? Well, parents do it too, only in a slightly different way. They aren't nervous for themselves, they're nervous that their little girl is headed out into the dark night with a stranger. (Or at least that's how they see it.)

So sometimes, to ease the tension, and in an effort to keep you from getting too attached, they'll tease you about the guys you go out with. Now, making fun of guys is bad enough, but some parents will actually do it in front of the guy. Not to be mean, but just to get a laugh. Make it clear to your parents that no funny business is allowed when he shows up, or you'll have to take care of business.

Home-Court Advantage

Introducing your guy to your parents before a date is one thing, but inviting him to sit down and have a meal or hang out with them is a different story. And yet, it has to be done. But when should you bring a guy home to meet the fam? How soon is too soon?

One of the reasons it's so nerve-racking for a guy to meet your parents is that he's the visiting team. Your parents know the turf and the rules. Essentially, the ball is in their court. So your boyfriend has to play a really good game if he has any hope of getting to the championship round. You can do a little pregame coaching (without making it seem too obvious) to help him knock the ball right out of the park.

Coaching Tip №1: Give him all the info he'll need to play well. For instance, if you've invited him over for a family dinner, let him know who will be there so he can picture the dinner in his head beforehand and maybe even think of a few conversation topics. He's going to be nervous enough as it is, so don't spring anything on him unless you have to.

Coaching Tip №2: If possible, level the playing field by doing pre-event introductions. Remember those embarrassing at-the-door moments with your mom and dad? They can actually come in handy if you're really going to date the guy. By having him meet your parents before he has to sit down and socialize with them, he can at least visualize who they are and how they will act.

Coaching Tip №3: If there's a special tradition your boyfriend is going to encounter during this first-time (or anytime) meeting, warn him. Is your mom making her special strudel for the holidays? Tell him, so he can compliment her cooking. How else will he know the strudel isn't standard fare around your house?

Half-Court Coaching Tip: During the parent meeting (a.k.a. dinner or party), help your guy out by throwing conversation topics his way and participating in the discussion. Bring up movies you know everyone likes, or say something like "Dad, Adam saw your new road bike in the garage and was saying how cool it is." It's always a good idea to get people talking about happy subjects—things they all like. (Hint: You can totally use this when you meet his parents, too!)

No Boyfriend for You!

Remember that classic *Seinfeld* episode about the Soup Nazi? If someone came into his deli and ordered soup the "wrong" way, he commanded, "No soup for you!" Well, sometimes it's the same with your parents. If they don't approve of a guy, they can be pretty harsh. But, "No boyfriend for you!"? It doesn't exactly work that way.

Most of the time, parents don't approve of boys for one of four reasons:

1. *They think you're too young to have a boyfriend.*
2. *They think he's too old to be your boyfriend.*
3. *Forget the specific boy. They don't want you dating one-on-one.*
4. *They think he's a bad influence.*

But you can get through this and find some common ground between your parents and your man. *Here's how:*

1. You know how, in romantic comedies, the heroine is always saying that age doesn't matter? Maybe it doesn't matter in the movies (or when you're 30) but, unfortunately, in high school, age *is* an issue. According to a lot of parents, if you can't drive—or at least hold a permit—you can't date. If this is your problem, see #3.

2. If the issue is that your boyfriend is an accused cradle-robber, there's not much you can do. I mean, it's not like you can suddenly skip two years of your life and be the same age as he is. (And really, you wouldn't want to. You've got two more years to live it up!) What you can do is give your mom and dad a chance to get to know him for him, not just how old he is. Have your guy over to the house so your parents can

GIRL TALK:

Keeping Him a Secret

"I never tell my mother when I have a boyfriend. I would be afraid she would freak out and never let me go out with him."
—Jolynn, 17

see why you're so into him. If that doesn't work, you might have to try being friends until you're eighteen and in college. And by then, you'll probably like someone else anyway.

3. Remember the big section on group dating in chapter 4? That's your answer. Group dating is the way to get out and about without actually "dating." You can still hang out with your crush and have a great time—it's just that there will be a few other people around. As long as your group-date-mates are friends, both you and your parents will be satisfied.

4. If your parents think your man is a bad influence, they must have some specific concerns, and you'll have to find out exactly what they're worried about before you can deal with anything. Do they think he's monopolizing all of your time? Do they think he's taking advantage of you in some way or pressuring you to do things you aren't ready for? Figure out what they're really freaking out about and then, if you think their fears are unfounded, tell them why. This is one of those times when nothing helps like a good old-fashioned heart-to-heart. (Hint: Do it over ice cream or dinner outside of the house so you all have to act like adults. No one can freak

ADVICE FROM SOMEONE WHO'S BEEN THERE

"It's always great when your guy and your parents get along; it makes for an easier time all around. At the same time, though, my parents have always been really overprotective, so no one was ever good enough for their little girl. I have never thought this was fair, and it tends to make me really defensive of my guys and relationships." —Anna Marie, 20

out at the local Olive Garden, and you just might get more talking done that way.) If you come out of the discussion realizing your parents have a point, consider yourself lucky to have gotten out of a close-call situation before it was too late.

Role Reversal: When You Meet His Parents

You know how protective your parents are of you? Well, your boyfriend's parents are probably just as bad with him. But that doesn't mean it has to be torture getting to know them. How could they not love you?! To get ready for the first meeting, take all the earlier advice in this chapter for helping your guy adjust and apply it to yourself. Here are a few extra hints to really get in good with the parents.

Make a good first impression. When your boyfriend introduces you to his parents, shake their hands and say how nice it is to meet them. First impressions are really important, since they tend to stick in peoples' minds long past second and third meetings. But don't let that scare you. Remember, nothing goes further than a smile when you're trying to make a good impression, so just grin and bear it!

Give 'em a hand. Nothing impresses parents more than offering to help out around the house. If your boyfriend has you over for dinner, offer to help clear the table and do the dishes. It will only take a minute, but the good karma will last for years. Parents love a girlfriend who seems responsible and is willing to do her share.

Make regular appearances. If you'd like this guy to stick around, it will help to be on his parents' good side. That way, if he comes home late for curfew because he was dropping you off, his parents will at least know it was for a good cause and might go easy on him. But in order to stay on their good side, you'll need to be around occasionally. That doesn't mean you need to live at his house. Just stopping by or hanging out there every once in a while will do the trick.

Hands off. He looks so cute in that ratty CBGB T-shirt, you want to run over and jump him. Just don't do it in front of his parents. They probably feel the same way your parents do about displays of affection (they don't like them), so keep your lovey-doveyness to a minimum until they're out of the room.

EXTRA CREDIT

Look the Part When You Meet His Parents

First impressions are really important, remember? Which is why you want to look perfect when you meet your boyfriend's mom and dad for the first time. But that doesn't mean you have to turn all Pollyanna or get decked out red-carpet style to make them like you. Just be yourself and remember these four little fashion hints:

1. Leave the cleavage. Meeting the parents isn't the best time to flash your "assets."

2. Heels aren't for inside the house. Your stilettos are totally stylish, but be sure to take them off at the door so you don't leave marks on the wood floors.

3. Make sure your feet are fab. Since you'll probably be taking your shoes off, make sure your socks aren't holey and your feet don't have that sweaty, sockless smell. Sure, your boyfriend's feet probably reek, but it's his house.

4. Don't sacrifice your personal style! His parents are meeting you, so make sure they get to meet the real you, leopard-print sweater and all.

You're No Prince Charming Yourself

I dated my fair share of guys in high school, and there was only one parent who didn't like me. (That I know of.) And he REALLY didn't like me. I think it had something to do with the fact that I was his son Carter's first official girlfriend. Or he was just a miserable old man.

I'd been going out with Carter for a few months, spending as little time as possible at his house, and then the holiday formal rolled around. At my school, the holiday dance was girls' choice, so I asked Carter. I was wearing a fab black designer dress with cutouts in the shoulders, sky-high black stilettos, and elbow-length gloves. I looked hot! Carter was going to find me irresistible!

I pulled up in front of his house, leaving my friend and her date waiting in the car. The door swung open after just one knock, and there was his dad, the devil himself, standing in the doorway.

"Well," he said, hand still on the doorknob, "if it isn't Cruella de Vil."

I paused. Did he really just say that?

Yes. He called me Cruella de Vil—as in the evil lady who wanted to kill 101 Dalmatian puppies to make a coat—to my face. And Carter was standing right behind him.

At the time, I was horrified and near tears. Looking back, I feel sorry for Carter. His dad is such a jerk that he'll probably never get a decent girl. (As far as I know, he still hasn't.) You'd better believe I didn't stick around after that. Carter was nice enough, but couldn't even stand up to his dad when I was getting ridiculed. I can only imagine what he would've called me at senior prom.

chapter 8

BOY FRIEND VS. BOYFRIEND

During my senior year of high school, I liked one particular guy. Or at least I thought I did. Then he asked me to prom and I realized that I did like him, just not like that. If I had figured that out before he asked me to prom, we might still be friends. But not all guys take rejection well. He accused me of leading him on. And my other guy friends gave me a hard time and said I was playing around with him.

I never wanted to lead him on, and I definitely wasn't trying to get him to fall in love with me. But I genuinely had a good time hanging out with him. He was a good study partner and the perfect person to call when I wanted company for a Jamba Juice run or coffee break. But did that mean I wanted to spend prom with my arms around his neck while we slow-danced to cheesy songs from the '80s? No way.

Once you're old enough to date, the word *friend* takes on a whole new meaning, especially when it comes to boys. But just because boy/girl relationships are more complicated now than when you were playing in the sandbox together doesn't mean you can't still live in harmony. (Can't you hear the birds singing?)

Just a Friend

"He's just a friend." We've all heard that one. But there are two sides to every friendship story. Does *he* think you're just friends, or is he hoping for something more? How can you tell if your favorite platonic playdate actually wants more from you?

Flip back and take a good hard look at the flirting chapter. Then ask yourself: Is he suddenly touching you more or finding reasons to spend more time with you? Those are big warning signs. And chances are that if he's flirting, there's a reason. Most guys don't put extra effort into someone they aren't interested in, even if you are a really great friend!

IF HE'S . . .

1. *Making up reasons to be alone with you*
2. *Referring to himself as your "boyfriend" but acts like he's joking*
3. *Acting jealous of your other guy friends*

. . . THEN YOU'VE PROBABLY GOT A CRUSH ON YOUR HANDS.

If you sense your guy friend is crushing on you, but you don't feel the same way, you've got to act quickly to save the friendship.

Situation One: He Hasn't Actually Said He Wants to Be Together

This is one of the only situations when it's a good thing that he hasn't said how he feels. It means that you can drop hints without blatantly rejecting him, and there are a few ways to do this.

First, make it clear how much you value him as a friend. You don't want him to think you're suddenly abandoning the friendship, but you do want him to understand that you don't think of him that way. One good way to spell this out is to tell him he's basically a brother to you. He should get it because no girl wants to date her brother. (Yuck!)

Then, if he's still dropping hints, try setting him up with someone else. Getting him interested in another girl is a good way to get his attention off you.

MY BOYS: THE PERKS OF BEING ONE OF THE GUYS

Remember Elaine from *Seinfeld*? Sure, she dated Jerry a long time ago, but really she was just one of the guys—and she liked it that way. Being one of the guys can be a lot better than having one of them as a boyfriend! You don't have to worry about all the little problems that come with romantic relationships, and you know you aren't going to lose a friend due to a breakup. You can just have a good time and count on the fact that your friendship will probably last a lot longer than the month-long relationships high school guys are famous for.

Situation Two: He's Professed His Love

This is a hard one because you have to acknowledge his feelings but let him down easy at the same time.

Start off by listing all the things you like about him—tell him, for example, that he's a great listener and your favorite running partner. And tell him that those are the reasons you would never want to jeopardize your friendship. Not only that, but you really see him as one of your best friends and you just don't know if you could look at him another way. Remember, your friend really put himself on the line by sharing his real feelings. The best way to respect that is to talk to him face to face, awkward as it might be.

Then, you need to give him some space. Depending on what kind of guy he is, he might act hurt or he might act angry. But either way, he's going to need some time to deal with your rejection. Ask if you can call him the next day, or tell him you're free Friday night and suggest that hanging out, but let him make the next move. After all, it's his heart that's just been broken.

Oh, and out of respect for your friendship (and the fact that he's a real person with real feelings), don't blast it all over school that he's in love with you. You don't want to embarrass the poor guy!

Most guys will eventually get over it and be able to be friends again. But if he becomes mean or resentful, consider yourself lucky to have discovered his true nature before you became even better friends. You don't need some bitter boy making your life miserable.

GIRL TALK:

Friends Make the Best Boyfriends

"My boyfriend was my best friend for like two years before we got together. It's cool because there was none of that weird getting-to-know-you stuff." —Joy, 16

FIVE REASONS WHY GUYS CAN BE REALLY GOOD FRIENDS

1. They don't care if you're wearing gold earrings, a silver belt, and brown shoes. And they definitely don't care what label your jeans are. No fashion pressure whatsoever.
2. They can give you an inside look at the mysterious male psyche.
3. They like to eat. Wendy's, anyone?
4. Most guys are pretty loyal. Once a good friend, always a good friend.
5. As much as you love your gal pals, it's nice to get a break once in a while.

Right Back at You

Of course, the "he's just a friend" situation can be reversed, too. Sometimes, after hanging out with a guy you think is super cool, you start crushing on him. And why not? You probably have a lot of things in common, like the music you listen to and the movies you like. But those in-between stages can be hard to navigate. Are you really into him or do you just like the idea of being into him?

If you've ever wondered whether your lab partner might want to go to the movies next Friday night, you're in boy-friend limbo. Take this quiz to figure out how you're really feeling. If the boyfriend category fits, you've got your answer.

THE BOY FRIEND VS. BOYFRIEND TEST

If you aren't sure where things stand with a certain guy, check out this comparison chart to see if he's true-love or just-friend material.

Situation	Boy Friend	* Boyfriend *
When you two have a conversation, it's usually about . . .	Anything that comes up. You can go on and on with him, but you can't really remember what you last talked about.	Something that you two unexpectedly have in common, like how you both love the Beatles before John Lennon got together with Yoko Ono, or how you're both dying to see the Galápagos Islands one day.
You run into him at a school dance, and you're both with other people. You think . . .	I'm so glad he's having a good time with Melissa!	He looks amazing in that tux. Just think how cute our picture would be if I were with him.
When he mentions another girl, you . . .	Try to picture them as a couple and give him some advice on how to get her to go out with him.	Feel like someone sucker-punched you in the stomach.
A girl from school asks you if you're dating him because she's kind of interested and doesn't want to step on your toes. You say . . .	We are SO not together. You should go for him. (And you mean it.)	I'm not sure if he's really your type.

Gimme More

You've determined that you want more from your guy friend than just a basic friendship. Now you've got to decide if you're willing to risk the friendship (and your feelings) by taking things to the next level.

Telling a boy how you really feel about him can be totally nerve-racking. After all, unless he's already come out and said he's crazy about you, it's hard to know what he's really thinking.

That said, are you willing to just sit around and act like his friend for the rest of your life, or would you rather know if there's a chance for you two? Nothing ventured, nothing gained. And it's not like you have to come out and say "I love you," all at once. Take it slow.

Start suggesting activities for just the two of you—not official dates, but normal hanging out, like watching the season finale of your fave HBO show or the Oscars. If he goes for it, you're on the right track. Pay attention to how he reacts when you're with other guys and if he seems interested in any other girls. You can tell a lot by just watching someone in a group.

As you start spending more time with him and show interest in him as more than a friend (e.g., hugging him good-bye, calling a little more often, etc.), you'll be able to tell if there might be a future. If he seems to reciprocate the interest, then you can suggest going out on an official date or tell him you think you might like him as more than a friend. Otherwise, if it seems like your feelings are a one-way thing, you can move on. (And yes, I know moving on can be hard, but there are lots of great guys out there. He's not the only one.)

The key to managing any "friend" situation is to go at your own pace. Who knows? He might make a move before you even have a chance, or you may fall in love with his best friend in the meantime. Either way, the experience is going to help with your guy interactions in the future.

EXTRA CREDIT

Four Fun (Nonthreatening) Activities to Help Create a Spark:

1. **Go ice-skating.** A lot of skating arenas are open even in the summer (which can actually be more fun than hanging out in a cold ice rink when it's freezing outside). Don't fret if you're not the next Michelle Kwan. No Olympic gold medals or triple axels needed at this rink. In fact, hanging onto his arm so you don't fall down (or vice versa) is a great way to get some close contact.

2. **Check out the video arcade.** It's just old-school enough to be cool. Pac-Man and Crazy Taxi are two of the best games ever made—guaranteed good times for you AND him.

3. **Go to the batting cages.** Since most guys like to be active, this is a good way for just the two of you to get out and do something. You don't need a whole team for this sport. Plus, he'll be impressed to see you knock it out of the park! Who could resist a girl like that?!

4. **Make a movie.** It doesn't have to be a feature-length film to be fun! Borrow your parents' video camera or use a Webcam and film a documentary on a day in the life of the two of you! Head out on the town to get some good footage. The best part is that you can watch it again after he goes home and see if your stomach butterflies go crazy or not—another good boy friend vs. boyfriend test.

chapter 9

BREAKING UP IS HARD TO DO

Have you ever noticed that A LOT of the songs on the radio are about heartbreak? Unfortunately, it's a common problem, and one that you will probably face more than once in your life. Unless you seal the deal with your boyfriend by taking a walk down the aisle (a word of advice: Don't do it yet!), you will more than likely break up with your current man at some point. But does that mean you should give up on love altogether? No way! Heartbreak is part of the equation, but you shouldn't have to miss out on all those cute "thinking of you" texts and great make-out sessions just because he might break up with you someday—or vice versa.

I know what you're thinking: The great parts of a relationship don't necessarily make it any less painful when the love of your life breaks it off. And you're absolutely right. But there are ways to make it through the breakup blues.

Boys Suck

You thought you loved him. And then the jerk breaks up with you for the new girl who transferred from prep school. What's your first thought? Revenge, of course. But as much as he might deserve a swift kick in the you-know-what, you can't go there. And you really don't want to. You aren't going to feel this way forever, and you don't want some heat-of-the-moment craziness following you into your next relationship.

The main problem is that after those intense feelings of revenge, sadness usually sets in. The phrase "love hurts" takes on a whole new meaning when you have feelings for someone and it turns out to be a one-way situation. Don't try to fight your feelings. (But it's totally understandable to wait until you're alone to get upset—it's not something the whole world needs to see.) A good cry or two will actually help you get over him. Why? Because, as cheesy as it sounds, once you've let yourself acknowledge how you really feel, you can start moving on. And the sooner you start moving on, the better. There's a whole planet full of guys out there!

Five Classic Songs for Getting Over a Guy

- **I Will Survive** by Gloria Gaynor. Cake's version is good, too. (Sing this one when you're getting ready for a much-needed GNO.)

- **You're So Vain** by Carly Simon (I listened to this over and over while writing this chapter!)

- **You Oughta Know** by Alanis Morissette (the boy-bashing anthem)

- **I Will Make You Cry** by Nelly Furtado

- **Love the One You're With** by Crosby, Stills, Nash, and Young

Heartbreak: It's Not All in Your Head

Think you're taking the breakup harder than your ex? There might be a reason for that. In a WebMD.com article on teen stress, Benjamin L. Hankin, assistant professor of psychology at the University of South Carolina, Columbia, says, "If there is a romantic fight between a boy and a girl, on average, a girl will respond with more depression. A boy will go distract himself," probably with something like sports or hanging out with friends. Just keep an eye on yourself. Depression that lasts longer than a few days isn't normal, and you should talk to someone.

Liar, Liar, Pants on Fire

You can't talk about breaking up without acknowledging one very big cause of breakups: cheating. As much as every mom would like to believe her son is a little angel, there are those guys who see nothing wrong with flirting with another girl while texting *love you* to you.

But before you kick a cheater to the curb, make sure you both agree on what constitutes cheating.

Girl Friends

He's going to have friends. And yes, some of these friends are going to be girls. And even if it makes you a little jealous, his talking to another girl does not qualify as cheating. (You talk to other guys, don't you?) But if he talks to another girl all night on the phone after telling you he's going to bed early? That's crossing the line and definitely worthy of a what's-going-on-with-you-two conversation.

MySpace Cheating

How do you know if your man is a MySpace player? Just check out his page. Do girls make up more than 50 percent of his friends? And are they practically naked in their photos? Does he act like he's hiding messages when you're around? Chances are, he's trouble. But if he lists you as one of his top friends, is mostly friends with people you know, and is open about having a girlfriend, you probably have nothing to worry about.

Kiss (Not the Metal Band)

Kissing another girl is cheating. If he's kissing you, he shouldn't be kissing anyone else. End of story.

CELEB SHOUT-OUT!

"If a guy isn't that into me, then I'll move on. I'm not wasting my time on that!"
—Amanda Bynes, actress

Four Big-Loser Boys to Avoid

(If you're dating one of these now, break it off—fast!)

The Mooch: This boyfriend asks you to and/or lets you pay for everything from his Mountain Dew in the cafeteria to gas for his car. Not only is he totally selfish, but dating him can get really expensive.

The Two-Faced Monster: You'll know you have this boyfriend if he acts one way in front of you and another way in front of his friends. At first you might think he's just being shy about dating you, but beware of someone who isn't proud of a girl as cool as you from the get-go!

The Suction Cup: This guy is also known as the Togetherness Terror. He can't even decide what kind of ice cream to get without your help, and sometimes you feel like he needs you so much that the life is getting sucked out of you. Tell your overly needy guy to grow up and think for himself!

The Jealous-Rager: If a guy gets jealous when you hang out with your friends or talk to another guy, he's out of control. Not only can a guy this possessive be scary, but he'll cut you off from everyone else too. If he can't accept the fact that he's not the only person in your life, he shouldn't be in your life at all.

Go Kind of Easy on Him

As much as it hurts to get dumped, sometimes being the one putting an end to things can be just as hard. Even though you're tired of being attached to one guy, bored with his dumb jokes, or starting to crush on someone else, you still don't want to hurt him. But don't feel bad that you're ready to move on—you're young, and this is the time to date around and try things out.

If you decide you're not really "in like" with your current guy, just be sure you take the high road and let him down easy. Think of how you'd feel if you were getting the heave-ho, and be as nice as you can.

GRANT ON ... Guys Getting Their Hearts Broken

For the first few years of high school, I never officially broke up with anyone. I just kind of stopped calling girls if I wasn't into them anymore. (Mean, I know, but I was a stupid guy.) But then I started dating this girl I was totally in love with. For some reason, her friends didn't think I was right for her, and she broke up with me. For days after, it felt like I was in a daze. I couldn't focus on anything, and I felt completely numb. It was awful. Anyone who says guys aren't affected by breakups is lying. I was like a walking zombie for a few weeks.

CELEB SHOUT-OUT!

"The bottom line is, why would a girl want to be with someone who doesn't want to be with her?"
—Kelly Clarkson, singer

"The reason I broke up with [my ex] wasn't to be with someone else—that's not why I did it. I felt like I needed to be by myself to learn about myself and to make decisions about what is best for me."
—Hilary Duff, actress

We Need to Talk: The Exit Strategy

Like any situation that involves people's feelings, ending a relationship can get really sticky. So how do you keep things as pleasant as possible?

First of all, unless you're dating long-distance, you should have a real conversation, either in person or by phone—face-to-face is definitely the best way to do it. DO NOT break up by e-mail, IM, or text. AOL and the Associated Press say that 13 percent of teens break up over IM. Seriously? Talk about being immature, not to mention a total wimp. Having the guts to say how you feel shows that you really care about the guy and that you're enough of an adult to keep it nice.

Plus, think about all those times you've misread an e-mail or text. Just imagine how "I don't think we should see each other anymore" is going to sound when he reads it on a computer screen.

Seven Signs You're Ready to Break Up

1. You roll your eyes when he calls to say good night.
2. You give your phone number to the guy at the grocery store.
3. You tell your best friend you won't talk to her ever again if she nominates you for cutest couple in the yearbook.
4. You see him flirting with another girl and you aren't jealous—just pissed that he isn't madly in love with you and only you.
5. He buys you two concert tickets for your favorite band and you wonder if you have to take him.
6. His name pops up on IM and you log out before he can message you.
7. You tell your mom not to call him your boyfriend.

Tips from Hotties Who've Had Their Hearts Broken

"Don't break up at school. He doesn't want everyone to see you dogging him." —Alex, 17

"Make sure you really want to break up before you do it. I'm not taking you back." —Aaron, 17

Maroon 5 singer **Adam Levine** disagrees: "You might break up with someone and realize, 'Oh, my God, I made the biggest mistake of my life—what was I thinking?' If that happens, I believe you can repair your relationship and get back together. But you only get one 'get out of jail free' card. Then, if you break up again, it's really over, and you know it wasn't meant to be."

"We aren't stupid. He probably knows you're about to do the deed before you do it. So just make it quick and get it over with." —Christopher, 18

Actress Amber Tamblyn has been on the receiving end of an e-mail breakup. What did she think about it? She told *Teen People*, "I think it's totally cheap and lame." No surprise there. You wouldn't want to get an e-mail like that, would you?

The second thing to remember when you're breaking up with someone is to be honest but brief. You have to own up to the fact that you don't want to date him anymore, but does he need to know that you have a crush on one of his friends? Not really. Keep unnecessary details that could hurt him to yourself, and hope that the next time he breaks up with someone he'll do the same. Maybe you'll start a breakup pay-it-forward trend. Here's to hoping all breakups will be as nice as yours!

Most importantly, when you're ending things, think of the Golden Rule and don't do anything to a guy you wouldn't want him to do to you. Guys might not always follow this principle, but that doesn't mean you shouldn't. Breakups don't always have to be nasty.

EXTRA CREDIT
Whether you were the breaker or the breakee, there's nothing like a little movie therapy to help heal your heart after a hard breakup. So call your BFF, buy some mint-chocolate-chip ice cream, and stock up on at least two of the seven all-time-best breakup movies.

1. *High Fidelity*
2. *The Eternal Sunshine of the Spotless Mind*
3. *Say Anything . . .*
4. *All the Real Girls*
5. *Better Off Dead*
6. *The Wedding Singer*
7. *The Break-Up* (can't have a breakup-movie list without this one!)

chapter 10

GETTING BACK IN THE GAME

There's an old saying, "If at first you don't succeed, try, try again." The same goes for dating. If at first you don't find the guy of your dreams or a relationship doesn't work out, don't give up—try again. Dating is a learning experience, and even though getting over someone is hard, once you do, you're that much smarter for the next go-around.

The Ex-Files

Whether you're the one who did the heart-breaking or you got your heart handed to you on a platter, running into an ex probably won't top your list of things to do. And yet, if you live in the same town (or even if you don't), you never know when you'll come face-to-face with the guy your friends refer to as "He who shall not be named."

But even though you may want to dive behind the nearest tree, the more put-together and confident you are, the better the run-in will be. For you at least. There's nothing worse than seeing your old Prince Charming and walking away feeling like you've made a total fool of yourself.

The initial spotting of the ex can be traumatic, but take a deep breath and force eye contact. Chances are he's probably seen you already (guys are like hawks when it comes to looking at girls), so avoiding his gaze will just make you look insecure. Your next move depends on the situation.

If you're across a crowded room or across the basketball court at a game, a short wave and smile will suffice. No need to start a conversation unless you have to. But if you run smack into each other, you should at least say hello.

If he's alone or with guy friends: This is the simplest of all the possible run-in scenarios, but that doesn't mean you want to make it any longer than it needs to be. A nice "What have you been up to?" is all you need to ask, and if you know his friends, a quick hello would be a polite gesture, too.

MOVE ON

After surviving a really public breakup with Jessica Simpson, Nick Lachey said, *"You can't let what happened in a previous chapter of your life dictate what happens in the next chapter of your life."* Well said, Nick.

GIRL TALK:
The Dreaded Ex Run-In

For the first few months after we broke up, I tried to look cute every time I left the house, thinking I would randomly run into my ex-boyfriend. Then, after I figured I would never see him again—he went to a different school—I saw him at the grocery store. And of course, I was wearing yoga pants and a baggy sweatshirt—not exactly the 'I want you back' image I wanted to give. But I smiled anyway and asked what he was up to. And then after we said good-bye, I turned down an aisle and caught him totally checking me out. I was just like, YES!"
—Marie, 17

If he's with another girl, introduce yourself but leave out the fact that you used to date the guy she's with. Instead, make a joke about where you are (the crowd, the weather, anything) to ease the awkward silence, and then say you have to run. (But don't actually run, even though you might feel like it!)

If you're with another guy, it might be tempting to throw your new hottie boyfriend in your ex's face, but instead introduce the two of them and leave your current boyfriend status out of it completely. (Better to leave the ex wondering!) Ask your ex how he's been, and once you've given him a chance to ask how you are in return, take your leave.

For the exit, a simple "take care" or "good to see you" is a gracious way to say good-bye and make it clear the conversation is over. Then, when you're out of his line of vision, give yourself a big grin. You came off looking great, and he's probably wondering why he's not still with you. There's nothing like leaving a guy wanting more!

But just because you aren't over him yet doesn't mean you never will be. Give yourself more than a few days. Remember on *Sex and the City* when Charlotte said it usually takes twice as long as the length of time you actually dated to get over a relationship? That's just one theory (keep reading for another), but the idea is a good one—take your time! Hang out with your girlfriends. Read that new book that's been sitting on your nightstand for the last six months. Design your own Web site. Do whatever it is that makes you feel better, and eventually you will be ready to head back into the dating world. Just don't mope around for too long. He might have been great, but no one is worth losing yourself over.

Getting Back in the Game Doesn't Necessarily Mean Getting Back Together. Sure, recycling is good for the environment, but when it comes to guys, try to remember why you threw him out in the first place before jumping back into a relationship with him. Getting back together will probably just generate a relationship repeat.

Six Signs You're Still Not Over Him

1. You constantly check your e-mail and phone to see if he's sent any messages.
2. Whenever "your song" comes on the radio, your eyes get watery.
3. Sometimes, when you pick up the phone to call your best friend, you accidentally dial his number.
4. You can't bring yourself to throw away that picture of him in his favorite baseball hat.
5. Your friends try to hook you up with other people, but you still compare everyone to him.
6. When strangers ask if you have a boyfriend, your first instinct is to say yes.

EXTRA CREDIT How Long Will It Take for You to Get Over Him?

Solve the following equation to get a sense of how long you need to really get back on the dating scene.

T = The amount of **TIME** you were with him, in months
(for example: one year = 12 months)

E = How much you were **EXPECTING** the breakup, on a scale of
1 to 3 (1 = "you broke it off," 2 = "you knew something wasn't
right," and 3 = "you were totally blindsided when he ended it")

L = Were you in **LOVE** or **LIKE** (2= "in love," 3 = "in like")

(T x E) / L = The average amount of time (in months) that it will
probably take for you to get over the guy

GRANT ON ... Moving On

After breaking up with a girl, a lot of my friends will start dating again right away. If this happens to you, don't be offended. It doesn't mean the guys aren't hurting, it just means they want to take their minds off things with someone new. Unlike a lot of girls, most guys don't want to take a trip down memory lane after things are over. Why hash it out if it's already done? (That's something else to keep in mind—don't break up with a guy unless you really want to. Most guys take things at face value.) To get over breakup pain, we like to get out and do something about it.

CONCLUSION

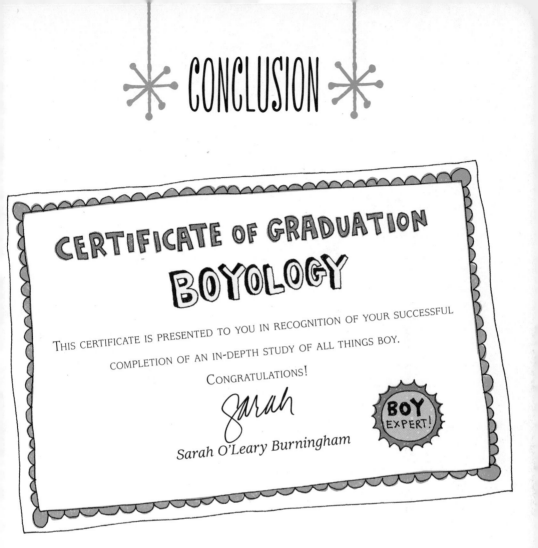

CERTIFICATE OF GRADUATION
BOYOLOGY

THIS CERTIFICATE IS PRESENTED TO YOU IN RECOGNITION OF YOUR SUCCESSFUL

COMPLETION OF AN IN-DEPTH STUDY OF ALL THINGS BOY.

CONGRATULATIONS!

Sarah

Sarah O'Leary Burningham

BOY EXPERT!

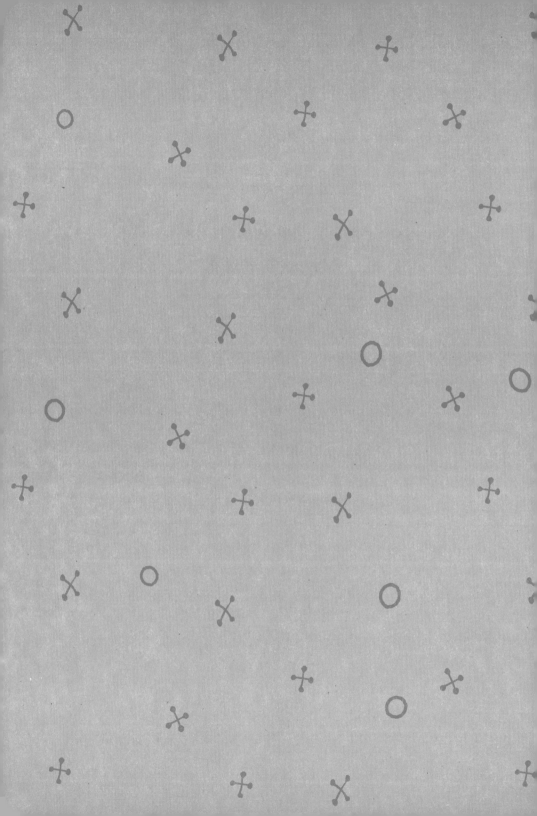

❋ ACKNOWLEDGMENTS ❋

This book is for my incredible husband, Grant, the man behind the "Grant on . . . " sections. He is the total Prince Charming package—handsome, smart, and funny. After years together, he still sends chills down my spine when he smiles. I love you, Grant.

I couldn't have written this book without all those amazing teenage girls and guys who shared their dating dramas, and real-life boyfriend/girlfriend experiences, and opened up about what dating and relationships mean to them. Thank you!

I also want to thank my parents, Dave and Julie, for their love and patience while I dated my fair share of boys. They (almost) always made me feel comfortable bringing guys and friends over, even though my dad's overprotective side made more than one boyfriend nervous!

My siblings (Annie, Katie, Jennie, and Connor) were total trouble-makers while I was dating. I caught them spying on me and my boyfriends more times than I can count (I was the oldest and the first one to bring boys home), but I think I got them all back when they were dating—so we're even! My brothers-in-law, Erik and Mike, survived their own initiations when they started dating my sisters and have been great "boys" to have around. My little brother, Connor, was great when it came to getting a guy's point-of-view, and I also have to give a little shout-out to his friend Winston. He's like another little brother and gave me tons of amazing advice about what dating is like for boys.

As with everything, my friends (especially Kathy, Chrissy, Bridget, Joy, Jill, Beth, Michael, and Kolt) were a great support. We had tons of fun conversations reminiscing about guys we had huge crushes on, losers we should've avoided, and guys who wouldn't give us the time of day. Although, it's beyond me why any guy wouldn't be interested in one of my fabulous friends.

This is the second book I've written with the help of incredibly talented editor Traci Todd, and I am still amazed by her endless creativity and fresh perspective. I also want to thank Julie Romeis, who inherited me after some reshuffling and never missed a beat. I am lucky to get to work with her and the rest of the wonderful team at Chronicle Books. Huge, huge thanks to publicity director Cathleen Brady, event coordinator extraordinaire Jessica Levy, and marketing director Chris Boral for their tireless efforts spreading the word. I'm the first to admit that I judge books by their covers, so lucky for me *Boyology* was designed and illustrated by true artists. Designer Amelia Anderson and illustrator Keri Smith are geniuses. Geniuses. My agent, Djana Pearson Morris, also deserves major thanks for working out all the nitty-gritty details and believing in this book from the start.

And of course, I have to thank all the guys I dated before I found Grant—they taught me all I know about the male species! From my first kiss on the playground to my first Homecoming date to my first real boyfriend to my first real love, I've been lucky enough to meet some great guys and they've all played an important role in this book.

❊ CREDITS ❊

Page 6
Emma Roberts. *CosmoGirl*, June/July
  2007.
Kirsten Dunst. *Thinkexist.com*.
Mae Whitman. *Thinkexist.com*.

Page 9
Zach Gilford. *Seventeen*.

Page 20
Amanda Bynes. *Ellegirl*, April 2007.
Mandy Moore. *People* magazine,
  July 9, 2007.
Adam Levine. *Seventeen*, August
  2007.
Ali Larter. *Thinkexist.com*.
Kelly Clarkson. *CosmoGirl*, August
  2007.
JJ Thorne. *Teen*, Summer 2007.

Page 37
Chris Evans. *CosmoGirl*, August 2007.

Page 43
Zach Gilford. *Seventeen*.

Page 49
Daniel Radcliff. *CosmoGirl*, June/July
  2007.

Page 54
Lauren Conrad. *Seventeen*, October
  2007.

Page 73
Vanessa Minillo. *Glamour*, July 2007.

Page 76
DJ AM. *Seventeen*.

Page 80
Avril Lavigne. *CosmoGirl*, June 2007.
DJ AM. *Seventeen*.
Enrique Iglesias. *OK!*, June 2007.
Adam Brody. *CosmoGirl*, May 2007.

Page 88
Sarah Jessica Parker. *TeenPeople*,
  March 2006.

Page 98
Iman. *CosmoGirl*, May 2007.
Fergie. *Seventeen*, June 2008.

Page 99
Zac Efron. *CosmoGirl*.

Page 106
Charles Peguy. *ThinkExist.com*.

Page 108
Fergie. *Seventeen*, June 2008.

Page 111
Brody Jenner. *Seventeen*, Dec 2007/
  Jan 2008.

Page 140
Amanda Bynes. *ElleGirl*, April 2007.

Page 142
Kelly Clarkson. *CosmoGirl*, August
    2007.
Hilary Duff. *Seventeen*.

Page 144
Amber Tamblyn. *TeenPeople*, April
    2006.
Adam Levine. *Seventeen*.

Page 148
Nick Lachey. *Etonline.com*, 2007.

✳ INDEX ✳

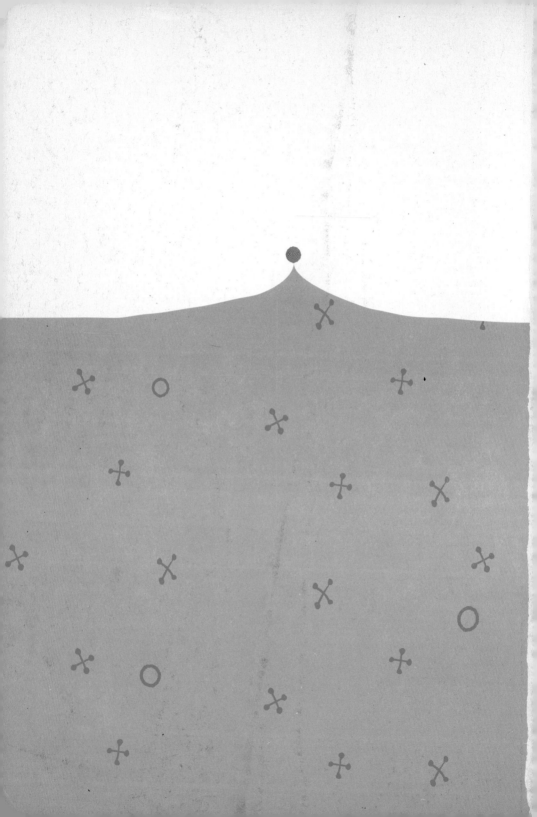